TOP GUN

50 YEARS OF NAVAL AIR SUPERIORITY

★ DWIGHT JON ZIMMERMAN ★

motorbooks

DEDICATION

To the late Robert F. Dorr, who served his country as a US Air Force pilot and State Department diplomat and honored me by allowing me to become his friend.

Brimming with creative inspiration, how-to projects, and useful information to enrich your everyday life, Quarto Knows is a favorite destination for those pursuing their interests and passions. Visit our site and dig deeper with our books into your area of interest: Quarto Creates, Quarto Cooks, Quarto Homes, Quarto Lives, Quarto Drives, Quarto Explores, Quarto Gifts, or Quarto Kids.

Inspiring | Educating | Creating | Entertaining

First published in 2019 by Motorbooks, an imprint of The Quarto Group, 100 Cummings Center, Suite 265D, Beverly, MA 01915 USA.
T (978) 282-9590 F (978) 282-2742 www.QuartoKnows.com

Motorbooks titles are also available at discount for retail, wholesale, promotional, and bulk purchase. For details, contact the Special Sales Manager by email at specialsales@quarto.com or by mail at The Quarto Group, Attn: Special Sales Manager, 100 Cummings Center, Suite 265D, Beverly, MA 01915 USA.

10 9 8 7 6 5 4 3 2 1

ISBN: 978-0-7603-6354-6

Library of Congress Cataloging-in-Publication Data

Names: Zimmerman, Dwight Jon., author.
Title: Top Gun : 50 Years of Naval Superiority / By Dwight Jon Zimmerman.
Description: Minneapolis, Minnesota : Motorbooks, 2019. | Includes index.
Identifiers: LCCN 2018053649| ISBN 9780760363546 (hardcover + jacket) | ISBN 9780760363553 (ebook)
Subjects: LCSH: Naval Strike and Air Warfare Center (U.S.)--History. | Fighter pilots--Training of--United States.
Classification: LCC VG94.6.N385 Z56 2019 | DDC 359.9/450973--dc23
LC record available at https://lccn.loc.gov/2018053649

Acquiring Editor: Zack Miller
Project Managers: Alyssa Bluhm and Dennis Pernu
Art Directors: James Kegley and Cindy Samargia Laun
Cover Design: Juicebox
Page Design and Layout: Kim Winscher

Printed in China

CONTENTS

INTRODUCTION

Whether you spell it "Topgun" (the Navy program) or *Top Gun* (the 1986 movie), the image evoked by the term is the same: that of elite US Navy fighter pilots—the best of the best.

Top Gun, the blockbuster movie that starred Tom Cruise, Kelly McGillis, and Val Kilmer—along with, of course, the F-14 Tomcat—exposed the wider public to the United States Navy Strike Fighter Tactics Instructor program.

The effect was sudden: every young male, athletic or not, who left the theater wanted to be a Navy pilot. And the Navy was there to take them, having set up mobile recruitment stations outside nearby to sign them up right then and there. And while there was a natural dropoff over the years, just the mention of the name "Topgun" is enough to catch the attention of young men.

In 2019, the Topgun program will celebrate its fiftieth anniversary. But the history of Topguns—fighter pilots who are the best of the best—has its origin in 1914 over the skies of Western Europe during World War I. In that conflict, brave men flew their flimsy fabric-and-wood aircraft and dueled like aerial knights.

Their exploits seized the world's attention, a hold on the imagination that has never let up. The postwar decades saw changes to the aircraft, going from two wings to one, from fragile fabric and wood to sturdy metal, from an open cockpit to an enclosed one. They could fly faster and higher and with an ever-deadlier arsenal, but one thing remained the same: all were flown by the best men—and now women as well—this country had to offer.

That seems to be changing, though: drone technology has brought what once seemed impossible to reality. The time will come when fighter pilots as we know them will no longer fly.

For this reason, it is even more important to celebrate the rich history of Topguns, those fighter pilots from both the US Navy and the US Air Force, and their many contributions to history and fiction, from their beginnings in World War I to present day. We should understand what it takes to be a Topgun.

No single book can tell their story, but before the living chapter of their history closes, let us pause to remember and honor those brave men and women who earned the silver and gold wings on their chest, those who flew, fought, and, in too many cases, died, in the defense of our nation.

> The planes rise heavy from her whining deck.
>
> Then the bomb's luck, the gun's poise and chattering.
>
> The far-off dying, are her near affair;
>
> With her sprung creatures become weak or strong
>
> She watches them down the sky and disappear,
>
> Heart gone, sea-bound, committed all to air.
>
> —William Meredith, *Carrier*

Opposite: The Grumman F-14 Tomcat is the first American military jet fighter to have twin tails. Its advanced weapons control system computer is capable of simultaneously tracking up to twenty-four targets.

ACKNOWLEDGMENTS

My friend, the late historian Thomas Fleming, aptly wrote, "My favorite metaphor for writing a history book is the image of an author standing on the shoulders of dozens of previous scholars." This I have done. The writers on whose shoulders I stood range from anonymous officers and authors of since-declassified monographs, to those credited in US Navy reports, magazine articles, and books. The list of such individuals is long, and the reading of their works—particularly the Navy documents—was fascinating, fun, and, ultimately, humbling.

There are four people, though, who I must single out for gratitude. The first is my publisher, Zack Miller; were it not for him, this book would never have been written. His support and suggestions in the nascent stages of the project were invaluable.

Paul D. Mather graciously gave me permission to quote freely from his article on Airman George Johnson's unexpected adventure as an F-86 jet fighter pilot. His multiyear effort to track down Johnson is a tale of dogged persistence that anyone who writes history would appreciate.

And, to Dave Berke, Lieutenant Colonel, USMC (Ret.), I wish to express my deep appreciation for him taking time out of his busy schedule to be interviewed and to provide photos for use in this book. In him, because of his qualifications, I hit a gold mine of information, and this book is made richer for it.

Finally, there is a fourth person, someone whom I do not know, who nonetheless deserves my sincere thanks. That person is you, the one who holds this book in your hands. Without people like you, books like this one that seek to honor those who proudly served in our nation's military would never exist. Thank you.

Opposite: The variable sweep wings on a Tomcat are automatically controlled by a computer, with manual override provided. Normal sweep range is 20 to 68 degrees, with a 75-degree "oversleep" position, which is used for shipboard hangar storage.

1 "I FEEL THE NEED ... THE NEED FOR SPEED."

Lieutenant Pete "Maverick" Mitchell (Tom Cruise) gives a thumbs-up while in the cockpit of his F-18 Tomcat. Competition for the leading role in *Top Gun* included Sean Penn, Patrick Swayze, Emilio Estevez, Nicolas Cage, John Cusack, Matthew Broderick, Michael J. Fox, and Tom Hanks.

On May 16, 1986, in more than a thousand theaters across the country, American audiences flocked to see one of the year's most hyped movies. Produced by Don Simpson and Jerry Bruckheimer, directed by Tony Scott, and distributed by Paramount Pictures, *Top Gun* was a movie full of supersonic sound and speed, starring one of Hollywood's rising stars, the handsome and charismatic Tom Cruise, as well as the beautiful (but relatively unknown) Kelly McGillis. Would its preview's claims of thrilling, action-packed aerial dogfights and push-it-to-the-limit-and-beyond relationships on the ground play out as promised? Or would *Top Gun* turn out to be a big-budget bomb like the previous year's *Cutthroat Island* and *Revolution*? Advanced screenings had called for a major change in the original plot. And one nervous Paramount executive complained that there was "too much flying." Earlier screenings in New York and Los Angeles had garnered mixed reviews from critics. Now it was up to the people who mattered most—the paying customers.

Before that first weekend was over, everyone involved with the film knew they had a major hit on their hands. Opening weekend sales totaled $8.2 million, more than half the movie's $15 million budget. And that was just the start of *Top Gun*'s success. By the time the movie closed in theaters on December 11, 1986, it had grossed more than $179.8 million domestically, with another $177 million internationally, making it the highest grossing film of 1986. *Top Gun* was a blockbuster.

Its heart-pounding appeal began not with sight, but with sound. The movie opened with German composer Harold Faltermeyer's score, beginning with a steady synthesizer drumbeat regularly punctuated by the haunting chime of a synth bell, evocative of a monk tolling a church bell to warn a town of trouble. As the white letters of the title, opening credits, and text appear and sequentially fade against the stark black background, the musical tension and urgency build. This dissolves into the silhouetted closeup imagery of flight deck operations in progress on a US Navy aircraft carrier.

An elaborate martial ballet commences as pilot and flight crew prepare an F-14 Tomcat, because of its size and power called the "King of Naval Aviation," for takeoff. The musical score overlaps with the clamor of jet engines and dissonant vocal orders and instructions. Then, with a dramatic outthrust of his arm, a flight officer signals the launch. This triggers a powerful steam catapult. The raw, testosterone-powered music of Kenny Loggins's "Danger Zone" pounds over the soundtrack, accompanied by the afterburner roar of two Pratt & Whitney jet engines, and the 61,000-pound Tomcat roars off the flight deck and claws its way into the sky.

TOM CRUISE

Thomas Cruise Mapother IV (born July 2, 1962) made his film debut in *Endless Love* (1981). This was followed by roles in *Taps* (1981), *The Outsiders* (1983), and *Losing It* (1983). His lead role as Joel Goodson, a rich, high-achieving high school student in *Risky Business* (1983), put him on a path to stardom that was fully achieved three years later in the international megahit *Top Gun*. From that point, his career shifted into high gear, with lead roles in *The Color of Money* (1986), *Rain Man* (1988), *Born on the Fourth of July* (1989), *A Few Good Men* (1992), *The Firm* (1993), *Jerry Maguire* (1996), and the *Mission: Impossible* and *Jack Reacher* franchises, among others.

Nominated three times for an Academy Award, Cruise excelled in bravura roles, playing brash, overly self-confident characters with a few cracks of self-awareness in their polished armor. Married three times, he has three children.

After several disappointing films that had dimmed his later career, the release of *Top Gun: Maverick* may return Cruise to his roots and restore luster to one of Hollywood's biggest stars.

In the movie's most traumatic moment, a guilt-ridden Maverick holds the body of Goose, accidentally killed while ejecting from their out-of-control F-18 Tomcat. Originally, the accident was to be the crashing of their F-18 on the carrier. The US Navy requested that it be changed to a fatal ejection caused by a malfunctioning canopy release.

Maverick (Tom Cruise) and Goose (Anthony Edwards) are reprimanded by Topgun CO Commander Mike "Viper" Metcalf (Tom Skerritt) after violating rules of engagement during their first training flight that included buzzing the base's control tower. The two literally wind up in Viper's crosshairs on another training flight when Maverick violates the Topgun rule that emphasizes fighting as a team.

A popcorn-crunching action-adventure movie, *Top Gun* was based on the United States Navy Strike Fighter Tactics program, nicknamed Topgun. (Note that the movie spells it as two words, while the Navy uses only one word. For consistency, whenever the movie title is used here, it will be two words; the Navy program will be one word). The movie propelled the careers of Tom Cruise, Kelly McGillis, and Val Kilmer, spawned numerous knockoffs and satires, influenced fashion, caused naval aviation recruitment to skyrocket, and ended up defining the high-powered action-drama movie genre of the 1980s.

The movie's story is straightforward, with as much subtlety as the F-14 Tomcat, its main (and most exciting) prop. The plot centers on the rivalry between US Navy pilots Lieutenant Pete "Maverick" Mitchell (Tom Cruise) and

Lieutenant Tom "Iceman" Kazansky (Val Kilmer), the former a push-the-envelope pilot with an insubordinate reputation bordering on the dangerous, the latter generally regarded as the Navy's best fighter pilot, one who plays by the rules.

Maverick and Iceman meet at Topgun, then located at Naval Station Miramar outside San Diego, California (in 1996 it would be transferred to Naval Station Fallon in Nevada). Only the best of the elite Navy pilot and radar intercept officer (RIO) teams are selected for Topgun training. Although their commanding officer has reservations about their conduct, he recommends Maverick and his RIO, Lieutenant (junior grade) Nick "Goose" Bradshaw (Anthony Edwards), for the program on the basis of their flying acumen.

Maverick and Goose soon discover that they're on a whole new level. In his first flight, Maverick can only defeat his "enemy," an instructor pilot, by breaking two rules of engagement, a move that doesn't go over well in the after-action debriefing.

Later, the class is introduced to astrophysicist and civilian Topgun instructor Charlotte "Charlie" Blackwood (Kelly McGillis), whose looks arouse a good deal of interest from the class. Maverick tells about an encounter with a Soviet MiG where he flew inverted over the fighter and flipped off the pilot, piquing Charlie's interest. She starts seeing Maverick.

The movie's real focus, however, is on the pilots, their airplanes, and a rivalry between Maverick and Iceman that ultimately results in tragedy. During a dogfight under Topgun, Maverick and Goose's Tomcat suffers an engine flameout and loss of power, resulting in the fighter entering an out-of-control flat spin. Goose suffers fatal injuries when the two eject.

Blaming himself for Goose's death, Maverick considers retirement. His self-confidence is restored after "Viper," Topgun instructor Commander Mike Metcalf (Tom Skerritt), reveals that he flew with Maverick's father. He gives Maverick heretofore classified information that shows Maverick's father died not in disgrace, but as a hero. Maverick returns to Topgun and graduates, watching Iceman take the Topgun Trophy as the best pilot in their class.

Maverick and Iceman are deployed to the carrier *Enterprise* and quickly find themselves ordered to provide air support for a rescue operation of a stricken ship that has drifted into hostile waters. This sets the stage for the climactic battle that serves as the movie's dramatic showpiece.

While providing air cover, Maverick, Iceman, and another Topgun classmate, Lieutenant Rick "Hollywood" Nevin (Whip Hubley), engage a superior force of six MiG fighters. Hollywood is shot down, but Maverick avenges him by shooting down three MiGs, with Iceman nailing a fourth. This causes the remaining two MiGs to break off and head for home. Maverick and Iceman return to the *Enterprise* and receive a heroes' welcome.

The movie concludes with Maverick, having been offered his choice of assignments, returning to Topgun, this time as an instructor. There he reunites with Charlie.

Top Gun was inspired by Ehud Yonay's 1983 article in *California* magazine. The article focused on US Navy pilots training in the Navy Fighter Weapons School program, then based at Naval Air Station Miramar in San Diego County.

Producer Jerry Bruckheimer read the article and thought its story had the makings of a great action movie. He convinced his partner with the pitch that it was "*Star Wars* on Earth." Simpson was sold, but getting the right screenwriter proved more difficult, and they were turned down by several of the top industry names. Eventually, Jim Cash, a former writing and film history professor from Michigan State University, and his partner Jack Epps Jr. signed on to the project.

For obvious reasons, the producers needed the US Navy's help. The Navy charged a reported $1.8 million for use of its ships, aircraft and facilities—a bargain, all things considered. But the Navy also saw *Top Gun* as a potential recruiting tool, and only agreed to participate if it had script approval. Outside script approval is always a delicate issue with producers and studios, and they'll usually fight tooth-and-nail to avoid it. The most important script change demanded by the Navy was the nature of Goose's death. Originally, it was the result of a fatal crash landing on the carrier's flight deck. The Navy thought this would have been "bad optics," and demanded the circumstances of the RIO's death be changed. The result was an ejection seat accident during training.

The Navy didn't get approval on everything, though, and the movie features a number of factual errors that still inspire anyone who served in naval aviation to cry out mockery or outrage. A Google search of "list of errors in *Top Gun*" will show that quite a few have documented their complaints online.

The clashed reality versus cinema is epitomized in an incident involving a Navy officer, one of many used as background extras in the film, and director Tony Scott. During a break in one of the hangar briefing scenes (an error of setting, as such an environment would be too noisy for such a meeting), one of the officers approached Scott to complain about the unrealistic collection of patches on the actors' flight suits. Scott is reputed to have growled, "We're

KELLY MCGILLIS

Kelly Ann McGillis (born July 9, 1957) made her film debut as a young college student in *Reuben, Reuben* (1983). Her breakout role came two years later in *Witness* (1985), in which she played an Amish mother whose son witnesses a murder and is targeted by the mob. She received Golden Globe and BAFTA award nominations for that role. This was followed by the role of Charlotte "Charlie" Blackwood in *Top Gun*. McGillis would go on to act in both film and television productions, as well as on stage.

Married twice, in 2009 McGillis revealed she was a lesbian. Work following her film career included employment in a New Jersey rehabilitation center helping drug addicts and alcoholics. Presently she teaches acting in North Carolina.

Charlotte "Charlie" Blackwood (Kelly McGillis) encounters Maverick while delivering a lecture in a hangar at Topgun. An astrophysist and civilian Topgun instructor, McGillis's character was based on Christine Fox, who worked at Naval Air Station Miramar and later served as acting United States Deputy Secretary of Defense, the highest-ranking civilian woman to work at the Pentagon.

VAL KILMER

Val Edward Kilmer (born December 31, 1959) initially led an eclectic career typical of actors just starting out. It included roles in theatrical performances, television commercials, and TV shows. He even self-published a book of poetry.

His big break came in 1984 with the lead role of rock musician Nick Rivers in the action comedy *Top Secret*. This was followed by the lead role in the science fiction comedy *Real Genius* (1985). It was his role as Lieutenant Tom "Iceman" Kazansky in *Top Gun* that elevated him to major stardom. His next major role was that of singer Jim Morrison in Oliver Stone's *The Doors* (1991).

His prolific output in the early 1990s included roles in *Heat*, the acclaimed crime drama co-starring Al Pacino and Robert de Niro, and in the Western *Tombstone*. His role as lawman Doc Holliday in *Tombstone* led to playing Batman in *Batman Forever* (1995), the third film in the Batman franchise.

Continuing his desire to seek out a wide range of opportunities, in addition to on-camera roles in movies and television, he has also done voiceovers and worked in the theater. Divorced, Kilmer has two children.

This confrontation scene between rivals Lieutenant Tom "Iceman" Kazansky (Val Kilmer, left) and Lieutenant Pete "Maverick" Mitchell (Tom Cruise, right) reportedly reflected the real-life tension that existed between the two actors during filming. Kilmer later said in an interview that the apparent dislike was professional, not personal, done to give verisimilitude to their onscreen rivalry.

Maverick serenades Charlie at the officers' club. Because McGinnis was 3 inches taller than Cruise, she was in stocking feet and he wore boots fitted to add extra height in scenes where they were supposed to be standing.

not making this movie for fighter pilots, we're making it for Kansas wheat farmers who don't know the difference."

Epps's legwork for the script included attending unclassified classroom briefings at Topgun as well as flying in F-14s. All the actors who portrayed pilots and RIOs were also given rides in Tomcats (flying in the RIO backseat). Only Anthony Edwards didn't need a vomit bag.

Script changes are the norm in any production, and the final version often bears little resemblance to the first draft. Such was the case with *Top Gun*. The nature of Goose's death is one such change. Another arguably more important change followed.

Various actors recall that a lot of the dialogue was improvised. Two improvisations became the most talked

(continued on page 18)

Maverick and Goose in the cockpit of their F-18 Tomcat. Unmentioned in the film is Goose's actual name: Nick Bradshaw. Each hour of F-18 flying time cost the studio Paramount $10,000.

"TAKE MY BREATH AWAY"

"Take My Breath Away" is the most famous song on the *Top Gun* soundtrack. Written specifically for *Top Gun* by Italian DJ Giorgio Moroder (tune) and American songwriter Thomas Whitlock (lyrics), the song was performed by the American New Wave/synth-pop band Berlin. In that version, it went on to win the 1986 Academy Award and Golden Globe Award for Best Original Song.

Appearing on the *Top Gun* soundtrack album and as a single, both formats became top hits in the domestic and international markets. The album was such a success that, to this day, it has endured as one of the all-time bestsellers in pop music. Allmusic. com states that the album's hits "still define the bombastic, melodramatic sound that dominated the pop charts" of the 1980s.

(Most people don't know that Berlin was not the first act to record "Take My Breath Away." Another New Wave band, The Motels, had recorded a demo of the song, but Moroder opted for Berlin, feeling their style was a better fit. The Motels's version can be heard on their compilation album *Anthologyland*.)

(continued from page 15)

about. The first was in the hangar briefing scene in which Charlie Blackwood makes her entrance. Maverick explains to her the unconventional maneuver he performed with his F-14 during an encounter with a MiG. During his explanation, Iceman coughs, "Bullshit." Iceman's comment was improvised, and the other pilots and RIOs' reaction was a real response, not scripted.

Another such scene occurs at the conclusion of a car chase between Maverick and Charlie. After she confesses she doesn't want anyone to know she's falling for Maverick, he is supposed to make a verbal response. But Cruise forgot his line and ad-libbed the impulsive kiss. Director Scott loved the action so much he let it stand.

By far the biggest change in the film was that of the character of Charlie Blackwood. In this case, the change was *not* imposed by the Navy, but by Paramount, the studio. As originally written, not only did the McGillis character have a different name, but also a completely different personality: Kirsten Lindstrom, an air-headed groupie or (depending on the version discussed) a gymnast.

Reportedly, Dawn Steel, then the head of production at Paramount, refused to greenlight the project unless the character was made into a mature, intelligent woman. Orders were issued: make the change. But, replace Lindstrom with what? That's when serendipity intervened.

During one of their visits to Miramar, the producers and writers met Christine Fox, a civilian mathematician (call sign "Legs") who worked at the Center for Naval Analysis located across the hall from Topgun. Additional meetings were arranged, and the team had its replacement. Fox would go on to have a highly successful career in the Defense Department, eventually serving as acting deputy secretary of defense, becoming the highest-ranking woman to serve in the Pentagon before retiring from government service in 2014. Her stellar résumé also includes this glamorous footnote: she became the inspiration for McGillis's revamped character, astrophysicist Charlotte "Charlie" Blackwood.

Apocryphal or not, director Scott's comment about it being a movie for "Kansas wheat farmers" and not Navy pilots was spot-on. Many critics, though, regarded it as less a movie and more a big-budget recruitment film. In fact, that was the most common criticism of *Top Gun*. Were they right?

Historian Craig L. Symonds was the head of the history department at the US Naval Academy and a member of its Admissions Board in the 1980s. He recalled that, after the movie opened, "We read the essays of applicants who wrote about why they applied. By far the most common explanation was that they had been inspired by the movie *Top Gun*."

Recruiting for the Navy's aviation program jumped 500 percent over the previous year. And Naval Aviation wasn't the only program to get a boost—Navy recruitment jumped across the board. Recruitment for the Air Force and Marine Aviation also spiked.

When the first DVD edition of the movie was being assembled for release, Paramount contacted the Navy and offered to let it include a recruitment commercial in return for forgiving its outstanding bill of $1 million. The Navy's advertising agency recommended that such a commercial would be redundant, because the film itself was such a great recruiting tool on its own.

Indeed, scores of young men throughout the country walked out of theaters echoing the words of Maverick and Goose. Like them, they "felt the need—the need for speed."

TOP GUN
TRIVIA

- At Topgun, a $5 fine is levied on any staff member who quotes the movie.
- Director Tony Scott wrote an on-the-spot personal check for $25,000 to the Navy, the amount the commander of the carrier said it would cost to have his ship make an unscheduled maneuver that Scott insisted he needed. Reportedly, the check was never cashed.
- The F-14 flying sequences cost Paramount $10,000 per plane per hour of flying.
- Kelly McGillis (5'10") is taller than Tom Cruise (5'7"). In their closeups, she was either barefoot and he wore lifts, or she stood in a trench.
- The "Top Gun Trophy" featured in the film is a piece of Hollywood myth-making. No such trophy exists.
- The Navy only authorized two missile shots for the film. Used in the climactic battle, they were shot from several angles to give the appearance of multiple shots. Other missile shots were conducted using miniatures of both the airplanes and missiles. They were so convincing, the scenes even fooled the Navy, which launched an investigation to determine how many real missiles were shot.
- The cameras used to film the aircraft-POV flight sequences were built and mounted onto the F-14s by Northrop Grumman, the Tomcat's manufacturer.
- Tom Cruise had never ridden a motorcycle before *Top Gun*. He learned how to ride in the parking lot of House of Motorcycles in El Cajon, California.

- *Top Gun* was one of the first movies selected for the Cinema 52 project, in which a "Cinemanaut" watches a movie fifty-two times over the course of a year, compiling notes during and after each screening. A full report can be seen on www.cinema52.com. Among the trivia notes: Tom Cruise blinks 469 times and the word "the" is spoken 223 times.
- The "Russian" MiG aircraft in the movie (and at Topgun itself) are actually American F-5E and Tiger II aircraft made by Northrop Grumman.

2 /// THE ORIGIN OF TOPGUN

Pursuant to CNO message DTG241506Z July 1968, during the period 8 August–8 November 1968, a five member review team, directed by Captain Frank W. Ault, USN [redacted]/1310, NAVAIRSYSCOM, (AIR-001), conducted an in-depth review of the entire process by which the Navy's Air-to-Air Missiles Systems are acquired and employed in order to identify those areas where improvements can and should be made.

Thus, in the dry, acronym-filled text that is the military style, begins the fifty-eight-page report, with six appendices, officially titled "Report of the Air-to-Air Missile System Capability Review (U)." Its author, Navy Captain Frank Ault, lent his name to the document: "the Ault Report," as it came to be known, forever changed US Naval Air fighter doctrine and tactics.

Written during the height of the Vietnam War, the report sought to explain what was taking place in the skies over North Vietnam: supposedly inferior North Vietnamese pilots (in equally inferior Soviet-built MiG-17s and MiG-21s) were going toe-to-toe with the US Navy's best pilots flying McDonnell Douglas F-4 Phantoms and Vought F-8 Crusaders—and shooting them out of the skies at an alarming rate.

In World War II, the kill ratio for US Navy pilots was 14:1, meaning that, for every fourteen enemy planes shot down, the Navy lost one. In the Korean War, that ratio was 12:1. In the Vietnam War, it had fallen off the eastern face of Mount Everest: a shocking 2.5:1.

The Ault Report posed five hard questions:

1. Is industry delivering to the Navy a high-quality product, designed and built to specifications?
2. Are Fleet support organizations delivering a high-quality product to the CVA's [aircraft carriers] and to the forward area sites ashore?
3. Do shipboard and squadron organizations (afloat and ashore) launch an optimally ready combat aircraft-missile system?
4. Does the combat aircrew fully understand and exploit the capabilities of the aircraft-missile system? (Corollary question: is the aircraft-missile system properly designed and configured for the air-to-air mission?)
5. Is the air-to-air missile system (aircraft/fire control system/missile) repair and rework program returning a quality product to the fleet?

The short answer to all five questions was "Hell, no."

Admiral Thomas H. Moorer was chief of naval operations (CNO) when Captain Ault's report landed on his desk on January 1, 1969. The CNO is the Navy's

During the Vietnam War, the Navy recognized the need for an advanced air-to-air tactical fighter unit. That unit became Topgun. Here, a catapult officer signals launch and an A-4 Skyhawk screams down the deck of an aircraft carrier in the South China Sea in March 1965.

most senior officer and commander; during the Vietnam War, he had operational authority over all US Navy fleets. A highly decorated World War II pilot, Admiral Moorer was the commander-in-chief of the Pacific Fleet in 1964 when the Tonkin Gulf Incident occurred. He had ordered an investigation into the controversial action between US Navy destroyers and North Vietnamese gunboats that precipitated America's entry into the Vietnam War in 1965. And he had led the investigation into an even more controversial attack: the one by Israeli fighters on the USS *Liberty* in 1967, findings which were suppressed by President Lyndon B. Johnson. He was therefore no stranger to events and information that could strategically, and unpleasantly, impact national security.

As he expected, Captain Ault's report was a chapter-and-verse condemnation. The captain had a reputation for bluntness bordering on the insubordinate, and had run afoul of many a superior officer for it. But Admiral Moorer was a big boy. More important, his men were dying in combat or languishing in brutal POW camps; as CNO, he had the authority to order whatever changes were necessary.

Everything centered on two overarching questions: How had naval aviation fallen so far so fast? And what could be done to restore the United States's reputation ASAP as it was smack-dab in the middle of a shooting war? There were two inextricably linked answers to the first question : inter-service rivalry between the Navy and the Air Force, and the atomic bomb.

The US Army Air Force (as it had functioned as part of the US Army during World War II) dropped the atomic bombs on Hiroshima and Nagasaki. That action opened a new, revolutionary chapter in warfare, one the US Air Force was determined to control once it became an independent branch of the military in 1947.

Essentially, the Air Force proclaimed itself to be the first line of national defense, a role historically held by the Navy. The awesome power of the atomic bomb (and later nuclear missiles, also under Air Force control) had rendered conventional arms and tactics subordinate at best, and obsolete at worst. Also, the Air Force engaged in a bureaucratic attempt to achieve a longstanding goal:

ABOVE: Admiral Moorer (second from right) poses with other naval officers during a ceremony. To Admiral Moorer's right stands Admiral John S. McCain—Senator John McCain's father.

RIGHT: In 1969, Chief of Naval Operations Admiral Thomas H. Moorer was determined to improve naval air superiority across the board. "No matter how complex or how awesome you build the weapons of war," he said, "man is still the vital element of our defense team. Men make decisions, men fight battles, men win war."

OPPOSITE: An A-4 Skyhawk stands secured to the flight deck of the USS *John F. Kennedy* prior to launch in December 1969.

TOP LEFT: The Navy's top ace during World War II was Commander David McCampbell. Here, Commander McCampbell poses in the cockpit of his F6F Hellcat on board USS *Essex* in October 1944. The Japanese flags below his fighter's canopy rail signify twenty enemy planes he shot down. At war's end he would tally a total of thirty-four Japanese planes shot down; receiving the Medal of Honor, the Navy Cross, amongst other decorations, as well as early Topgun acclaim.

TOP RIGHT: Lieutenant Edward H. "Butch" O'Hare was another of the Navy's top aces during World War II. Here, he strikes a pose in front of his F4F Wildcat fighter in the spring of 1942. The destroyer USS *O'Hare* was named after him, as well as the eponymous airport in Chicago, Illinois.

LEFT: Three F-4J Phantom II fighters fly in echelon formation. The Phantom became operational in 1960 and was the Navy's primary fighter during the Vietnam War. It was the first warplane to be designed for a new style of aerial combat that emphasized fighting beyond visual range using air-to-air missiles.

F-4 losses occurred at unbelievable rates in Vietnam as they fought the North Vietnamese piloting MiG-17 and MiG-21 jets. Their adversaries' seemingly obsolete close dogfighting tactics rendered the Phantom's long-range air-to-air missiles mostly useless.

taking naval aviation away from the Navy and making it a part of the Air Force, thus making it the sole provider of American aerial warfare.

When North Korea invaded South Korea in 1950 and initiated the Korean War, the Air Force's theory and doctrine was put to a real-world test. By the time an armistice was signed in 1953, the doctrine was in tatters. The Korean War had revealed the all-or-nothing battlefield limitations of atomic warfare (to say nothing of the moral consequences to noncombatants), underscored by President Harry S. Truman's refusal to authorize use of atomic weaponry (to this day, Japan has been the only nation to suffer a nuclear attack). In addition, naval aviation's rapid-response capability in the early weeks of the war had blunted the North Korean Army's offensive, eclipsing to the Air Force's bureaucratic threat.

Senior naval officers could breathe a sigh of relief: their carriers were saved. But the dragon's teeth of complacency had been sown. Naval leadership was seduced by the siren's call for high-performance, jet-powered warplanes using radar and missiles that could engage enemy aircraft "beyond visual range," thus making obsolete the close-in dogfight tactics that had made heroic pilots aces (with five or more aerial shootdowns) in World Wars I and II and Korea. The new generation of jet warplanes exemplified by the McDonnell Douglas F-4 Phantom (operational in 1960) would no longer be armed with machine guns. Instead of such close-quarter arms, the fighters would carry longer-range air-to-air missiles like the Sparrow and Sidewinder.

In 1960, the Navy decommissioned its Fleet Air Gunnery Unit (FAGU), which had been responsible for developing fighter pilot training. This was the branch's recognition of a change in its doctrine, believing that knowledge of dogfighting tactics was no longer necessary. In addition, nonstandardization of fighter training became the norm. In the upshot of this change was that the Atlantic and Pacific Fleet squadrons received different training.

In post-FAGU training, exercises revolved around fighter pilots flying level at slow-flying, non-maneuvering drones. Once the pilot got into missile range—which was, per the new doctrine, beyond visual range—he would get a lock on the drone and fire a dummy missile at it. The goal was not to score a hit, but, for reasons of economy so that the dummy missile could be re-used, to achieve a *near miss*.

Then came the Vietnam War.

Navy pilots were operating with a combination of unrealistic training and highly restrictive rules of engagement. Flying their modern jet fighters into combat, they were poorly matched against North Vietnamese pilots, who used "obsolete" dogfighting tactics in their highly maneuverable (though "inferior") fighters to close in the envelope—ranges too close to effectively deploy Sparrow or Sidewinder missiles. Instead of being hunters, they became prey to gunfire from outmoded cannon and machine guns.

On November 1, 1968, President Lyndon B. Johnson acknowledged the failure of his Rolling Thunder bombing campaign of North Vietnam, and ordered a halt to bombing attacks above the twentieth parallel. This gave the Navy a much-needed opportunity to clean its bloody nose and reevaluate its fighter doctrine and tactics.

The change in approach began with the Ault Report. The 242 problem areas identified there included missile maintenance at sea (so poor that in many cases the missiles were rendered inoperable by sea and shipboard conditions), crews' unfamiliarity with missile capabilities, and, of course, aerial combat tactics.

LEFT: An F-4 Phantom takes off from the USS *Constellation* on a strike mission over Vietnam. When the first class of Topgun recruits went to war, Admiral Moorer and other officers, trainers, pilots, and crewmembers were nervous. Would it work? Could pilots learn never-before-taught skills, and pass those skills on to their fellow airmen? When Lieutenant Stephen J. Barkley returned from his first combat mission, he left the cockpit smiling—he had shot down a MiG-21. Topgun worked.

OPPOSITE: Admiral Moorer was no stranger to the need for discretion—and then action—when it came to military actions. Moorer led the investigation into the Israeli attack of the electronic spy ship USS *Liberty* in 1967—the news of which President Johnson tried to suppress.

You might think that, given events in Vietnam and the CNO's support, the new fighter pilot training program that came to be known as Topgun would receive the Navy's full support. And you would be wrong.

Truth was, the mere idea of Topgun threatened many powerful admirals and other stakeholders. While they couldn't stop the program, they provided it with less than full support. For this reason, until Topgun could prove itself, the program was largely on its own. As such, it needed a special leader for its first commander. That individual was Lieutenant Commander Dan Pedersen, a pilot in VF-121, based at Naval Air Station Miramar outside of San Diego.

Described as a movie studio's idea of what a fighter pilot should look like, Lieutenant Commander Pedersen had a big frame for a fighter pilot and exuded confidence that stood out even among the outsized egos that make up the fighter pilot community. An excellent pilot among excellent pilots, he also had a driving maturity to achieve. He would need both traits if he was to accomplish Topgun's goals.

At the time pilots slated for the F-4 received their final training at Miramar in what is known as a Replacement Air Group (RAG); in this case, it was VF-121, which made it logical to locate the new fighter weapons school there. When approached to take on the billet as the new school's commander, Lieutenant Commander Pedersen refused. He was slated to be VF-121's tactics commander, a highly coveted post at Miramar, and his first assessment of the command was of one surrounded by question marks and no's—no budget to speak of, no facilities, no staff, no planes. All-in-all, this big shiny idea had all the makings of a surefire career killer.

Upon reflection, all those negatives were what finally convinced Lieutenant Commander Pedersen to accept the position. His successful career had been based on taking on and overcoming challenges, and what particularly appealed to him was that no one had ever been responsible for both running a new school *and* developing new tactics. He became determined to make Topgun a successful graduate-level dogfighting school. But he didn't have much time: classes were scheduled to begin March 1, less than two months away.

LEFT: President Lyndon Johnson (center, in ball cap) and Secretary of Defense Robert McNamara (lower right) observe flight operations from the bridge of the nuclear aircraft carrier USS *Enterprise* off the California coast in 1967. Their fears that the war in Vietnam could escalate into World War III caused them to enact highly restrictive Rules of Engagement and micromanage all air operations over North Vietnam.

BELOW: The initial training location for the Navy's new advanced fighter pilot program—Topgun—was Naval Air Station Miramar, located north of San Diego, California.

F-8E Crusader pilots often referred to themselves as Top Guns. Here, a Crusader of All Weather Fighter Squadron 235 is loaded with 250-pound bombs and rockets for its next mission over Vietnam in April 1967.

With no budget and little official support, using a commandeered trailer for an office and classroom, Lieutenant Commander Pedersen and his assembled team of eight pilot and RIO instructors tossed out "the Book"—the existing training manual—and, with the Ault Report in hand, worked to distill its findings into the framework for a workable training program.

They also wanted to come up with a name for the school. Sure, it already had one: the United States Navy Fighter Weapons School, but that was the *official* name. Though it was descriptive, it wasn't sexy. When someone suggested "Topgun," the vote was a unanimous "aye." Why Topgun? The term had been in use for years by the Navy, referring to different things. It was the name for the annual Navy air weapons meet. The aircraft carrier USS *Ranger* was nicknamed the "Top Gun of the Fleet." F-8 Crusader pilots called themselves "Top Guns." And the Crusader's soon-to-be-decommissioned weapons school was referred to as "Top Gun." Now spelled as one word, a new Topgun chapter was about to begin.

As time was of the essence, they identified three points that would have the quickest impact: change the F-4

Phantom flight training, gather every scrap of intelligence that they could about their adversaries' MiG-17s and MiG-21s, and develop a new doctrine that emphasized the Phantom's strengths and exploited the MiGs' weaknesses.

Then responsibilities were handed out. Lieutenant Jim Ruliffson, who had a tour in Vietnam under his belt, had already proved himself to be a great instructor, having served as one in VF-121 for the previous two months. He had both an intimate knowledge of what made an F-4 tick and a knack for passing on his knowledge in a way that the listener could easily grasp.

Among all the pilots there, it was acknowledged that no one matched the skill of Lieutenant Mel Holmes. He had demonstrated an ability to make the F-4 do things no one

thought possible. Though others would assist, so he wouldn't have carry all the weight himself, Lieutenant Holmes's primary role at Topgun was to do something the Navy otherwise never would have allowed, owing to the danger involved: play test pilot for the Topgun syllabus.

Thanks to his experience in an F-111 fighter-bomber (which included a landing accident that broke his back and grounded him for a year), Lieutenant John Nash was tapped to develop the air-to-ground syllabus. He would also play the role of "aggressor"—an instructor teaching Navy pilots how to dogfight. As he had ached to get back to flying fighters, this was a chance to vent more than a year's worth of frustrations built up from cooling his heels on the ground. It was an opportunity he relished.

The term "Top Gun" had actually been used in the Navy for years. The aircraft carrier USS *Ranger* was known as "Top Gun of the Fleet," and F-8 Crusader pilots sometimes referred to themselves as Top Guns.

The F-111B Aardvark was the world's first production variable-geometry-wing aircraft. A multirole warplane whose variants ranged from strategic nuclear bomber to tactical attack aircraft, it was the result of a 1961 shotgun wedding between the Air Force and Navy as ordered by then–Secretary of Defense Robert McNamara, who believed he could save money by having a one-plane-fits-all requirement identified by the two branches. Though the two-branch goal didn't pan out because the F-111 proved impractical for carrier operations, the Aardvark had a long and successful career in the US Air Force. Introduced in 1967, by the time it was retired in 1998, it had fought in the Vietnam War, Operation El Dorado Canyon against Libya, and in Operation Desert Shield/Desert Storm.

They integrated analysis of the Ault Report with their own knowledge of the aircraft they flew. Though the Phantom had great power and thrust, superior climbing ability, and, at high speeds, was a deadly monster, most pilots were not aware of the F-4's top-end capability. Those who *did* know had been scared away from using it by McDonnell Douglas representatives who claimed such high-performance maneuvers were dangerous, would cause excessive stress on the wings, and, besides, the F-4 was an interceptor, not a dogfighter.

Lieutenant Commander Pedersen and his pilots knew otherwise: they had pushed the F-4's aerodynamic envelope beyond the manual's limits and lived to tell the tale. As for the fear of excessive stress (with the frightening and possible fatal consequence of having the warplane disintegrate), they discovered that the F-4 could take the punishing maneuvers and then some, at the minor cost of an occasional loss of slats or bent wings.

They didn't just rely on their own experience, either. Whenever the opportunity arose, they picked the brains of

other successful fighter pilots, not only in the Navy, but also from the Marines and Air Force. And they got out of the cockpit and went back to the drawing board, talking to the engineers who had designed the plane and anyone else who might have a kernel of information that might help.

That was one side of the training coin. Not exactly easy, but doable. The other side would be far more difficult: getting book on the MiG-17 and MiG-21. It wasn't as if they could call up engineers at Mikoyan-Gurevich headquarters in Moscow and place an order for the fighters and their training manuals, to say nothing of picking the brains of Red Air Force fighter pilots.

Lieutenant Commander Pedersen and RIO J. C. Smith went to Washington to see what they could find about the MiGs. They hit the jackpot in the top-secret bowels of CIA headquarters at Langley, where boxes of MiG-17 and MiG-21 specs were stored under heavy guard. They made regular flights back and forth from Miramar, laden with suitcases of documents they had laboriously copied. As these were commercial flights (and they wore civilian clothes), they were in a constant state of anxiety that something might waylay those suitcases.

Meanwhile, other pilots were doing their due diligence, talking to fighter pilots freshly returned from combat and scouring the base library for material.

Even so, there were still significant gaps in the intelligence they obtained, gaps that could only be filled by someone with proper security clearances—the kind possessed by an air intelligence officer. RIO Smith discovered that that one such person existed at Miramar, in the form of Charles "Chuck" Hildebrand, on temporary duty as a communications officer for a photo-recon squadron.

After doing a preliminary background check, RIO Smith arranged a meeting with Hildebrand and came away convinced that he was the man they needed for Topgun. Now the trick was how to get him. And for that, he pulled out a number in Washington Lieutenant Commander Pedersen had given him, not stating who belonged to that number, but that Smith was to only use it when absolutely necessary. If ever there was a situation, this was it. Smith

dialed the number and made his request. The person at the other end of the line said the transfer would be taken care of. An hour later, an astonished Hildebrand called RIO Smith and said that he had just received orders transferring him to Topgun. Smith put down his receiver, suddenly aware that some very serious muscle was supporting the fledgling program.

Hildebrand delivered what were probably the most important documents for Topgun: the after-action debrief reports on recent MiG engagements. Among his findings was that, naturally enough, North Vietnamese pilots were

A pair of Teledyne-Ryan Firebee II target drones mounted beneath the left wing of a Lockheed DC-130 drone control aircraft. The supersonic drone could also be launched from the ground using a rail launcher. It was capable of providing realistic target simulations for surface-to-air and air-to-air defense and interdiction training. A parachute was deployed following termination of the exercise, enabling the drone to be repaired and reused until it was totally destroyed.

using Soviet tactics. Those tactics had changed little since World War II, and they were rigid. Pilots were controlled by a ground-based headquarters that relayed all intercept instructions. The basic flight pattern was for the MiGs to fly nap of the earth to neutralize American radar. Then, when they had gotten into a position behind and below an American warplane, they would swoop up in a steep vertical, fire a quick tail shot once they got close, and then dive back to the deck and escape. These ambush "hit-and-run" tactics, as simple as they were, were effective and had made some of their pilots aces. One, Colonel Nguyen Toon (known as "Tomb") had reached legendary status.

As for the fighters themselves, the subsonic MiG-17, codename "Fresco," was roughly half the length and a third the weight of an F-4. This "aerial hot rod," as it was known, was hard to see, highly maneuverable, and its combination of two 23mm and 37mm nose cannons and Atoll air-to-air missiles packed a deadly punch for the close-in combat it was made for. The MiG-21 "Fishbed" was larger and faster, similarly armed, and equally capable for hit-and-run strikes.

The Phantom, on the other hand, was much easier to spot. In addition to being significantly larger, it also emitted a black tail of smoke visible as far as 20 miles away.

After reading all the reports, Lieutenant Commander Pedersen and his team identified patterns and began developing countermeasures. As their lesson plans to implement the new doctrine were coming together, one overarching fact kept bothering them. They had all kinds of information about the enemy fighters, but the one thing they didn't have was an actual MiG. That's when an astonishing breakthrough occurred. The February 1969 issue of *Aviation Weekly* contained a short article stating that the US Air Force possessed a MiG-21. Lieutenant Commander Pedersen and his men dug further and discovered the sister service actually had MiG-21s, plural, and MiG-17s.

The Navy had the doctrine, the Air Force the hardware. Strings were pulled, clearances obtained, and instructors and students went up to Naval Air Station Point Mugu in Ventura County where, under the auspices of VX-4 (a test and evaluation squadron), they were able to eyeball and then fly the planes they were learning to fight.

Because the MiGs, especially the MiG-17, could turn on a dime and fly at a speed so low a Phantom trying to match it would stall, every time an F-4 tried to follow a MiG into a turn, the Phantom immediately found itself outmaneuvered and being bounced by the MiG. Because the Phantom had more power and a superior roll rate, the engagement countermeasure adopted was to keep the MiGs at arm's length, at least a mile and a half. And, if things got too hairy, a maneuver called the "bug out" was created, in which the Phantom pilot horsed his F-4 in a perpendicular angle away from the MiG's line of flight. If that failed to do the trick, they developed the "depart," a last-resort maneuver using the Phantom's superior speed to "get out of Dodge."

They also devised a tactic that turned the strength of the MiG-17's superior turn rate into a weakness. The maneuver was called the "lag pursuit." Basically, the F-4 followed the MiG, keeping it at arm's length by staying behind and outside the MiG's turning radius.

Another tactic they developed was called "loose goose," in which a two-plane element did tag-team combat against a single enemy. Whoever spotted the enemy airplane first would lead the attack, with the other serving as wingman, regardless of who was the senior officer. This was a radical shift from the hierarchal Fluid Four doctrine practiced by the Air Force, in which the most junior wingman was not allowed to attack a bogey, even if he had the best shot.

In addition, as part of the program, students were using live missiles for the first time ever. Previously, everyone used nonmaneuvering drones. And, to keep costs down, pilots weren't allowed to hit their targets, just log near misses that counted as "hits" so that the drones could be retrieved and reused.

That changed with Topgun. Now they had real Sparrows and Sidewinders under wings and fuselage, and engaged Teledyne-Ryan Firebee II (BQM-34E) supersonic target drones that had MiG flight characteristics.

A MiG-21 (NATO code-name "Fishbed") of the Romanian air force takes off during an air show event in 2016. Introduced in 1959 by the Soviet Union (now Russia), the MiG-21 is still in service in a number of nations' air forces. Its reason for longevity is that it is cheap to build, fast (Mach 2), and easy to maintain. It proved a hardy foe in the Vietnam War and saw action in the Middle East, conflicts between India and Pakistan, and in the Iran-Iraq War. At one point, the American military purchased a squadron of the Chinese-built version (the J-7), which were used in aggressor training exercises by the Navy and Air Force, thus giving pilots an even better understanding of their potential adversary's capability.

There was a practical reason for this, coupled with a genuine fear: though pilots trusted in the Sidewinder, they had no faith in the Sparrow, whose failure rate in combat was off the charts. The only way to find out exactly what made the Sparrow tick and how to best use it was to do real exercises, not go-through-the-motion maneuvers that bore no relevance to combat conditions. The missiles didn't have explosive warheads, but they didn't need to: the kinetic energy coming off Mach 2 for the 7-foot-long, 5-inch-diameter Sparrow alone was more than enough needed to score a "kill."

Exercises took place over the Pacific Ocean, with the drone controlled by headquarters on the ground. Coming at the end of their training, this exercise was the payoff, and all the pilots looked forward to it. One of the pilots wrote, "They were so good that not only did they hit the drone with their first shots, but they also requested and got second and third drones sent up, even shooting missiles into the debris to watch them hit smaller parts."

Between test flying tactics and preparing the syllabus, Lieutenant Commander Pedersen and his team were putting in sixteen-hour days. Their effort resulted in a three-hundred-page syllabus that was a complete overhaul of fighter pilot doctrine. They changed air combat maneuver (ACM) tactics in addition to how RIOs used their radar. Among other things, this meant greater coordination and communication between the pilot and his backseater, something that had seriously lagged in previous years.

The program would last four weeks, with three weeks of air-to-air training and one week of air-to-ground operations. The new pilots in Miramar's RAG program were used to make up a first informal class—a test run, as it were. They loved what they were hearing. And, in the flight exercises, the new maneuvers gave both students and instructors the belief that the tactics had reversed the aerial playing field so that it overwhelmingly favored Navy pilots.

The first official class commenced on Sunday, March 3, 1969. It consisted of eight pilots and RIOs from VF-142 and VF-143 from the USS *Constellation*. The pilots

were Lieutenant Ron Stoops, Lieutenant Jerome Beaulier, Lieutenant Cliff Martin, and Lieutenant John "Pudge" Padgett. The RIOs were Lieutenant Jim Nelson, Lieutenant Jack Hawyer, Lieutenant Bob Cloyes, and Lieutenant Ed Scudder.

The purpose of the course was to teach the aircrews who would, upon their return, pass on the lessons learned at Topgun to their squadron mates prior to deployment. It wasn't a one-way program, either: this graduate course in ACM was going to be a learning experience for the instructors as well as the students. As such, the instructors encouraged feedback; after all, these were experienced pilots. Given the life-and-death stakes involved, the aircrews could be brutally blunt if they didn't like something, as an engineer from Raytheon discovered. After delivering an eyerolling, jargon-laden lecture on the complexities of one of the company's missiles, the Topgun students let him have it. Specs they could read. What they needed was information that would be useful in combat. Chastened, the engineer came back with what they were looking for.

Initially, "aggressor" aircraft, flown by the instructors, were Douglas A-4 Skyhawks and T-38 Talons, airplanes that had similar performance characteristics to the MiGs. The instructors would "attack" the students flying F-4s and, after soundly defeating the students, would then show the students how to perform the new dogfighting tactics. The pilots and RIOs emerged from that first class with enhanced confidence that they took back to their squadrons.

While that first class went off to war, Lieutenant Commander Pedersen and his instructors did an after-action review of their syllabus. When the second class arrived, a revised and updated program was in place.

It didn't take long for word to come back from Vietnam. On March 28, 1970, Lieutenant Beaulier made Topgun history. Flying an F-4J Phantom II from VF-142 with RIO Lieutenant Stephen J. Barkley, he shot down a MiG-21 Fishbed, making him the first Topgun graduate to shoot down an enemy airplane. Topgun training worked. Naval aviation was back on the path of becoming top dog in the air.

3 /// HOLLYWOOD JUMPS INTO THE COCKPIT

Protocol requires movie studios (or anyone for that matter) who wish to use a service branch's personnel, facilities, or equipment to obtain permission. But in the case of the RKO movie *King Kong* (the original 1933 release), protocol was told to pound sand.

In the film, a giant gorilla is captured on a remote island in the Pacific and brought to New York City for display—mayhem ensues. King Kong escapes and, in the climactic sequence, he battles a flight of US Navy fighters while standing on the Empire State Building before being gunned down.

Herb Hirst was the location manager for RKO. He wrote to the Navy requesting the use of four pilots and Helldiver fighters from the Navy's base at Long Beach, New York, for one day. To help pave the way for cooperation, Hirst stated that, in addition to paying all the Navy's expenses for the shoot, including insurance, he had already received permission. This permission, however, was for the Eleventh Naval District on the West Coast, where Hollywood was located—not the naval district responsible for New York City and environs—and was pending approval from the Navy's CNO. A copy of the screenplay was included with the request.

King Kong.

The CNO had turned down the request, "in that there is nothing pertaining to the Navy and use of planes as requested would compete with [the] civilian airplane industry."

But instead of ending the matter, the studio went around the CNO's office by meeting with the commander of Floyd Bennet Field on Long Island while shooting location scenes in and around New York City. In exchange for a donation to the Officers' Mess Fund and payment of the four pilots, permission was granted.

The three Navy and one Marine pilot selected were excited over the idea of buzzing the new Empire State Building, a skyscraper completed just two years earlier. Added to the thrill was the fact that military regulations prohibited flights of under one thousand feet. Thinking that the studio had received permission, the four pilots were determined to take full advantage of their once-in-a-lifetime opportunity.

The "attack" lasted less than fifteen minutes. Cameras were stationed at a variety of strategic locations, shooting footage that included scenes of the fighters flying in formation, peeling off for the attack, and executing various dives and sweeps at and around the Empire State Building.

AERIAL FOOTAGE

So, how does a movie crew film an aerial action/combat sequence? The short answer is that it all comes down to money. The more money available, the better the final product. Even then, it's anything but a cakewalk. The sequences take careful preparation and choreography before the camera starts rolling.

The biggest challenge facing any movie crew looking for exciting aerial combat action scenes is to make them believable. You can't get much more fake than scenes shot in a studio with a pilot reacting in his static-mounted airplane, pretending to engage in a dogfight in front of a blank screen where flying warplanes will later be projected.

A pilot who had served in World War I, director William Wellman solved this problem in *Wings* by giving the pilots in the film precise instructions on the maneuvers he wanted. And, with Army Air Service assistance, he managed to get a plane equipped with an airborne camera system that allowed him to get closeups of the pilots in flight.

The climactic air "combat" sequence in *Top Gun* presented numerous challenges as well. Former fighter pilot, racing pilot, and successful businessman Clay Lacey had modified a Learjet with special viewing windows in the fuselage and floor, equipped with high-quality movie cameras for film work.

Formation flying sequences in which the Tomcats were simply cruising back and forth through the air were relatively easy to shoot. The combat sequence, though, required special thought and planning. For safety reasons, rules require a minimum of five hundred feet of separation between aircraft. But footage shot under that protocol reduced the planes in action to literal pinpricks on the film. After much discussion between the pilots who had to perform the maneuvers,

the director, and the cinematographer, it was agreed to significantly reduce the separation distance and do other maneuvers the director requested. The next day they went up for the shoot. As film historian Lawrence H. Suid noted, "Such assistance enabled the filmmakers to create in *Top Gun* some of the most dramatic scenes of jet fighters in action that Hollywood was ever to put on the screen."

A Marine Corps Curtiss SBC-4 Helldiver, similar to the planes used in the original *King Kong*.

The Empire State Building was just two years old when it was used as a location in *King Kong*. Since then it's been featured in more than 250 movies and television shows. On July 28, 1945, a B-25 Mitchell bomber, flying low in thick fog, crashed into its north side. The Civil Aeronautics Administration subsequently ordered a minimum flying altitude of 2,500 feet over New York City.

Riding with the Marine pilot, Lieutenant John Winston, was an observer. Lieutenant Winston later said that, when he buzzed the skyscraper, he "got close enough to scare my observer." And no doubt all the office workers inside the building must have wondered what was going on.

It's not known how naval high command reacted once they learned they'd been hoodwinked, but they seem to have let it slide.

King Kong was the exception. In all other cases, studios played fair with their requests, sometimes with the military going out of its way to help for reasons of their own. What follows are some quick takes of the many movies in which the military officially participated.

Wings (1927). This silent film became the standard for aviation movies, with realistic air combat sequences that serve as the benchmark for all aviation films to follow. In the Academy of Motion Picture Arts and Sciences inaugural award ceremony in 1929, *Wings* received Academy Awards for Best Picture and Best Engineering Effects. In 1997, the Library of Congress selected it for preservation in the National Film Registry.

Directed by William Wellman, a World War I fighter pilot with three confirmed and five probable kills, it starred Charles Rogers, Richard Arlen, and Gary Cooper (his debut role) as pilots. Originally written as a straight war

The Curtiss JN4 Jenny was one of several types of biplane used in the movie *Wings*.

Famous for his swashbuckling roles in *The Thief of Bagdad, The Mark of Zorro,* and *Robin Hood* during the early twentieth century, Douglas Fairbanks was Hollywood royalty, the most famous actor of his day.

picture, the screenplay was revamped to shoehorn in Clara Bow, Paramount Pictures's most popular star, as a female love interest. It was shot on location at Kelly Field, then an Army Air Corps base near San Antonio, Texas. About three hundred pilots, many of them active duty, participated.

Released in August 1927, it quickly became a big hit, notable for the realism of its combat sequences and memorable for its release less than three months after Charles Lindbergh made his historic transatlantic flight from New York City to Paris.

The Dawn Patrol. A World War I movie about the dangers of air combat and the stress of command so good, they made it twice. The first version, in 1930, starred Douglas Fairbanks and won an Academy Award for Best Story. The 1938 remake starred Errol Flynn, the first film in Hollywood history to be honored with a "remake."

Iron Eagle (**1986**). One of a number of *Top Gun* knockoffs, this movie is notable for its totally implausible storyline. A high school teenager and his friends break into an Air Force base, steal an F-16, and the teenager then flies the fighter to a hostile Arab country to rescue his father. Oh, it also spawned three—count 'em, *three*—sequels.

THE WORLD WAR II SUBGENRE

World War II provided movie studios with something invaluable: actual combat footage from gun cameras in fighter planes and from cameramen shooting film while flying in bombers on missions.

One of the best movies to take advantage of that footage was Twentieth Century Fox's *Twelve O'Clock High* (1947), starring Gregory Peck as a squadron commander who becomes psychologically overwhelmed by the stress and pressure of command. Though a film about a B-17 Flying Fortress bomber squadron, the combat footage dramatically shows tiny German Bf 109 and FW 190 fighters zooming through the lumbering formations of the much larger bombers.

The movie was nominated for four Academy Awards, winning two (Best Actor in a Supporting Role and Best Sound Recording). Veterans of the heavy bomber campaign praised the film for its accuracy and realism, and it would become required viewing at all the service academies for many years. In 1964, it became a television series that ran for three seasons.

Flying Leathernecks, an RKO movie from 1951, starred John Wayne and Robert Ryan. It was another war movie that incorporated extensive combat footage, in this case color. The integration of color into this technicolor offering was relatively rare, as most World War II combat footage had been shot in black-and-white.

MOVIES AS PROMOTIONAL TOOLS

Top Gun was not the first film to be seen—or exploited—as a promotional tool by the military. Two earlier examples include the World War II drama *Flying Leathernecks* and *The Bridges at Toko-Ri*, set during the Korean War.

Flying Leathernecks tells the story of a Marine fighter squadron engaged during the Guadalcanal campaign. Logistics forced the studio to take liberties regarding warplanes. The actual planes that had fought in the battle, Grumman F4F Wildcats and Japanese Zero fighters, only survived in museums at the time the film was made. Instead, the studio used F6F Hellcats and Chance-Vought F4U Corsairs, the latter Marine fighters that only appeared later in the war. RKO might have used T-6 Texan trainers, which *did* exist in quantity and could be easily modified to resemble Zeros (a trick studios later used), but the studio opted to paint a batch of decidedly un-Zero-like Hellcats white, with large red "meatballs," large red circles on fuselage and wings.

Flying Leathernecks is noteworthy for serving as propaganda for the Marine Corps. Shortly after the Air Force became an independent branch, a movement swept through Congress, supported by the Army and Air Force, to disband the Marine Corps. Recognizing that its most effective battle in this bureaucratic climate was public opinion, the Marine Corps rolled out the red carpet to any studio doing

ABOVE: Grace Kelly was the most glamorous actress of the 1950s. She retired from acting at age twenty-six when she married Prince Rainier of Monaco.

TOP INSET: A poster for the 1951 movie, *Flying Leathernecks*. It was the first war movie to use color footage from a World War II fighter gun-camera, adding authenticity to the aerial combat sequences.

ABOVE: Charles Lindbergh became world famous for being the first pilot to make a nonstop, transatlantic flight in 1927. While serving as a civilian consultant for Corsair manufacturer Chance-Vought in World War II, he flew fifty combat missions and downed at least one Japanese plane.

RIGHT: The Boeing B-17 Flying Fortress was the most famous bomber in World War II.

movies that portrayed the Marine Corps favorably. *Flying Leathernecks* became one such movie to benefit from this support, and the studio received access to facilities and aircraft at Camp Pendleton in Southern California—anything the studio wanted, the Marine Corps gave it.

As a story, the movie is standard fare, remarkable primarily for its color war footage. Still, it was a movie at the right place at the right time; it helped serve the Marines's purpose (a little conflict called the Korean War also helped, but that's another story). The Marine Corps survived the Congressional budget axe.

The Bridges at Toko-Ri (1954), a Paramount Pictures production, had everything you could ask for in a movie about naval aviation and fighter operations: full cooperation from the Navy that included the use of *two* aircraft carriers; an all-star cast that included William Holden, Mickey Rooney, Frederick March, Grace Kelly, and Robert Strauss; color combat footage of the Korean War; *and* a good story. Based on the bestselling novel of the same name by James Michener, it is the story of naval aviation operations in the Korean War. Nominated for two Academy Awards, it won one for Best Special Effects.

Although the Navy loved the way the movie portrayed carrier aviation operations, even using it to help Congress increase its budget for carriers and jets, critics paradoxically noted that it was the first true antiwar movie to be released after World War II.

4 TOP GUN *IN PRINT*

OPPOSITE: Detail of an early 1940s pulp magazine cover illustration featuring aerial combat between stylized British RAF and German Luftwaffe warplanes.

RIGHT: Englishman Richard Horatio Edgar Wallace was one of the most prolific authors of the early twentieth century. At the height of his output, one of his publishers claimed that a quarter of all books published in England were written by him.

The real-life heroic exploits of fighter pilots created an insatiable popular demand, and the publishing industry was quick to capitalize on it.

English crime writer, journalist, and playwright Edgar Wallace was among the first. The guns of World War I were still firing when his short story, "Tam O' the Scoots," appeared in the November 1917 issue of *Everybody's Magazine*.

Tam was an RAF fighter pilot with a heavy Scottish accent (thus the "Scoots" for "Scouts," an early reference to fighter planes). He appeared in a variety of magazine short stories that were collected into an anthology published in 1918. The stories were light on accuracy and heavy on action and thrills. Young Charles Lindbergh was one of countless boys captivated by Tam's high-flying derring-do, inspired by dreams of becoming fighter pilots when they grew up.

Pulp magazines (so named for the type of wood pulp paper used to print them) were quick to jump into the fighter pilot cockpit, and such bestselling anthology fiction magazines as *Argosy*, *All-Story*, and *Blue Book*, among others, included action-filled fighter pilot tales. They were soon joined by magazines solely devoted to fighter pilots. Titles ranged from the literal (*High Adventure*) to the

Harry Grant Dart was a cartoonist and illustrator known for his futuristic, often aviation-oriented art. This drawing appeared on the cover of an issue of *All Story* magazine.

The XF5F Skyrocket was Grumman's proposal for a twin-engine fighter for the Navy. Despite excellent handling and speed, it was ultimately rejected by the Navy. Its only "operational use" was that by the Blackhawks in their Quality Comics comic book series.

lurid (*Molly & McNamara: Satan's Playmates, Sky Devil: Hell's Skipper*).

Arguably the most successful in the genre was *G-8 and His Battle Aces*. Launched by Popular Publications (which dominated the genre) in 1933, each issue of the monthly series contained a novel-length story. The magazine ran for 110 issues over an eleven-year period that ended in 1944.

Its hero is the mysterious English fighter pilot and spy known only by his code name, G-8. His intrepid wingmen are two Americans, Nippy Weston and Bull Martin. G-8's manservant, Battle, and an unnamed nurse love interest

round out the supporting cast. Ongoing villains were the mad scientist Herr Doktor Krueger, the Steel Mask, and Grun.

"The Bat Staffle," the title of the first G-8 story, a fast-paced blend of spy thriller, horror fantasy, and aviation adventure set the tone for the series. G-8 is given the mission to stop Herr Doktor Krueger from releasing poison gas over Allied lines from German aircraft resembling giant bats (the "Bat Staffle").

G-8 attempts a solo attack against the Bat Staffle but winds up on the losing end. He is saved from death by the intercession of pilots Weston and Martin, who wind up

(Continued on page 51)

With covers featuring bright colors and lurid action, *G-8 and His Battle Aces* and *Dare-Devil Aces* were typical of the sensational fiction magazines offered during the Pulp Era.

PULP-ERA NEWSTANDS

Newsstands during the Pulp Era, generally considered from the late 1890s to 1950, were the analog equivalent of today's Internet. Whatever the interest, topic, genre—you name it, there was a magazine for it.

During their heyday, the decades of the 1920s and 1930s, most pulps came out weekly or bi-weekly, with others published monthly. Publisher Frank Munsey's *Argosy Magazine*, released in 1896, is considered the first pulp magazine. With prices ranging from ten cents (average) to twenty-five cents (considered expensive), circulation of the top-selling titles such as *Argosy*, *Adventure*, *Blue Book*, and *Short Stories* numbered in the millions. At their peak, more than 150 different titles were available.

Pulps began to decline after World War II for a variety of reasons, not the least being the new entertainment medium of broadcast television. By 1960, they had literally shrunk to digest size and only a handful, mostly science fiction and mystery titles, remained. By the 1980s, even those were gone.

Argosy All-Story Weekly was an enormously popular weekly fiction anthology. Launched in 1882 as *Argosy*, it was the first pulp magazine. During its extraordinary ninety-six-year run, the magazine published novel serializations and short stories of all types. Among its many authors were Tarzan creator Edgar Rice Burroughs, mystery writers Rex Stout, and Mary Roberts Rinehart, and Western writer Max Brand.

(Continued from page 47)

becoming his wingmen. The trio then embark on a series of hair-raising, death-defying attempts to stop the Bat Staffle and destroy the poison gas.

The series was written by Robert J. Hogan who, unlike most pulp fiction authors, used his real name for his work. He was born in 1897 and was a pilot in the Army Air Service (as it was called in World War I). After his discharge, he became an airplane salesman. Unemployed as a result of the Great Depression, Hogan read a fighter pilot story in a pulp magazine and was convinced he could write better. He moved to New York City to become a pulp fiction writer, selling his first story in 1932. He continued writing after the G-8 series ended. He died in Florida in 1963 at age 66.

The advent of World War II saw the launch of a new line of aviation pulps, with fighter pilots flying more modern (in some cases, futuristic) fighter planes. Among the first to jump into the modern fighter cockpit was *Captain Bill Combat*.

American pilot Bill Combat suddenly finds himself thrust into the new and terrible war that's broken out in Europe when the Nazis murder his mother and uncle. Released in 1940, well before America's entry into the war, *Captain Combat* was a three-issue series, with each issue containing a novel-length adventure.

Dusty Ayres and His Battle Birds, another successful popular title, departed slightly from the typical military aviation fare found in pulps in that his stories were set in the not-too-distant future and in a world war in which the United States stood alone against enemies that held most of the world under their bootheels.

The fate of the free world rests on the shoulders of Dusty Ayres and the intrepid pilots of his squadron. Created by Robert Sidney Bowen Jr., a former World War I ace, the series debuted in 1934 and ran for twelve issues. Bowen went on to write a popular adventure series for boys, the *Dave Dawson War Adventure Series*.

Though comic books had existed for a few years, they were "born" in 1938 when Superman debuted in *Action Comics* #1. When World War II broke out the following year, the comic book industry was quick to go to war as well,

in fifty-two-page, all-in-color-for-a-dime issues. Following the Japanese attack on Pearl Harbor, Hawaii, that plunged America into war, the comic book industry went on a war footing of its own, releasing war-themed titles ranging from fictional stories to biographical battlefield accounts, with titles that focused on a specific military branch. One of the most popular heroes was the mysterious fighter pilot Blackhawk, leader of the international Blackhawk Squadron.

Debuting in *Military Comics* in August 1941, the Blackhawk adventures were limited only by the imaginations of its writers and artists. At its peak during the 1940s, it outsold all other comics other than those starring Superman.

Reed Crandall was the series's artist during the war. One day he found a pair of FBI agents at the door of his Long Island studio. It turned out that the airplane he was drawing in his Blackhawk adventures bore a suspiciously accurate resemblance to Grumman's XF5F-1 Skyrocket, an experimental naval fighter. The agents wanted to know how he got such accuracy in his drawings, particularly from their many angles.

At one point during the meeting, the three heard the engine roar of a low-flying aircraft. Looking out the studio's window, they saw a Skyrocket from Grumman's nearby airfield performing aerial stunts as it conducted a test flight over Long Island Sound. The agents politely excused themselves.

The 1940s are regarded as the Golden Age of Comics. By far, the greatest number of military and fighter pilot comic book titles were produced in that time. By the 1960s, the fighter pilot subgenre had all but disappeared, with two notable exceptions by Superman and Batman publisher DC Comics: Captain Johnny Cloud, a Navaho fighter pilot flying a P-51 Mustang in World War II, and Hans von Hammer, a German fighter pilot flying mostly the Fokker DR 1 Triplane.

Though all had notable runs, with many stories rising above the typical comic book fare, particularly Gorge Pratt's 1990 original graphic novel *Enemy Ace: War Idyll* about the last days of Hans von Hammer, by the 1980s the war subgenre in comics had all but vanished.

5 /// SO YOU WANT TO BE A FIGHTER PILOT

In the wake of *Top Gun*'s release, a long line of hopeful young men took a shot at becoming fighter pilots, blissfully ignorant of how long the odds were—longer than the lines they stood in at the recruiting office!

Recent numbers illustrate the difficulty of making the cut. More than 16,000 young men and women applied to enter the US Naval Academy in Annapolis, Maryland, in 2017. Of that group, about 1,100 were accepted; 240 of those midshipmen were accepted as pilots, and eighty out of those 240 were accepted into the jet training program. Finally, only fifty men and women succeeded in becoming fighter pilots for the US Navy.

All fighter pilots and most military pilots are commissioned officers, citizens of the United States, and all start out at the entry-level rank of ensign (Navy) or second lieutenant (Marine Corps, Army, Air Force, Air National Guard). (Some helicopter pilots can be warrant officers, a different category that isn't relevant here.) Pilots must have at minimum a bachelor's degree (in any major) with at least a "B" average. Regarding age requirements, the minimum age is eighteen and, though the maximum age varies slightly between branches, a pilot must be commissioned before

reaching the age of twenty-eight. Upon earning his or her wings, the pilot must agree to serve for eight to ten years.

Many, but not all, military pilots get their start by attending one of the service academies. Flight training begins after academy or college graduation at a branch's aviation schools, which are located in a variety of locations in the West and South. Typical classroom courses include aerodynamics, aviation weather, aircraft engines and systems, navigation, flight rules and regulations, and so on. Flight training itself has a number of progressively more complex stages, beginning with simulators and propeller-driven trainers and advancing up to jet simulators and trainers.

Throughout this process, doctors conduct a very thorough medical screening of each student aviator to ensure the person is in excellent health, has perfect eyesight, and is free of all allergies, in addition to confirming the candidate's physical suitability to sit in a cockpit.

Even if a student aviator has the mental chops to become a fighter pilot—or any kind of pilot in the military, for that matter—that intellectual skill will be irrelevant if the student's body isn't prepared. That can happen in one of two ways, or both.

Air combat maneuvers put enormous stress on the human body. Wearing a special pressurized suit, a pilot

OPPOSITE: US Naval Academy midshipmen taking their oath of office at graduation ceremonies on May 25, 2018. Future Navy fighter pilots are included in this group.

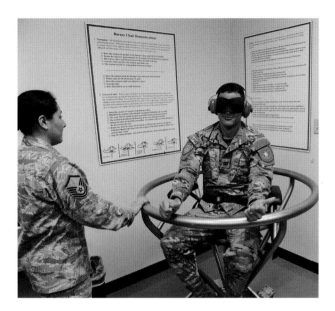

can endure a gravity force (g-force) of up to eight or nine g's. (This can be compared with the maximum g-force of six g's experienced on an amusement park ride.) The baseline measurement is one g, which is the weight you normally feel. To test an aviator's ability to withstand such stress and maintain equilibrium, each student undergoes a motion-sickness test in a "multi-station spatial disorientation device," the Bárány chair, referred to by all of its survivors as the "spin-and-puke chair." Though it invariably takes more than one session to get used to the g-force, those who can't endure multiple sessions without vomiting their guts out will wash out of the program.

The body's anthropomorphic measurements can also disqualify a student aviator. Aircraft cockpits come in different shapes and sizes. While they must have perfect 20/20 vision, stand between 5'4" and 6'5" tall, and not be overweight, the student aviator's specific body dimensions must also fit certain criteria. Length of limbs should be within a certain range, as should the seating distance. There are many other body measurements that must conform, and if the body isn't a proper fit for a fighter jet

cockpit, there is no appeal: the aviation student is out of the fighter program and has to hope his or her body shape falls within the parameters of one of the other airplanes in the service's inventory.

Training takes about two years. A candidate who passes has truly earned his or her wings and becomes a member of an elite group.

To recap, becoming a fighter pilot or other pilot in the military requires that the candidate:

- Pass all academic tests
- Receive commission (or earns a warrant rank)
- Undergo about two years of training
- Spend hours in flight simulators and flying with instructors
- Spend more time flying solo in different trainers
- Pass all flight examinations
- Conform to physical specifications and passes all medical tests

If all these criteria are met, then voilà, you're ready to fly in the fighter of your dreams.

Or, you could be George R. Johnson of the US Air Force.

Not an officer, Airman First Class Johnson was simply an enlisted man. He didn't have a college degree, just training from the service's technical schools. He was an airplane mechanic working to get a civilian pilot's license; at the time, had a total of just two hours in the air, flying with an instructor in a Piper Cub.

For one hour on the night of September 20, 1956, though, Johnson was a jet jockey flying one of the Air Force's frontline fighters, the F-86 Sabre.

Johnson grew up loving airplanes and dreaming of being a pilot. Inferior eyesight rendered that career path impossible. If he couldn't fly the planes, at least he could fix them. He volunteered for the Air Force and trained as an airplane mechanic. Part of maintaining and repairing the Sabre's systems was also to sit in the fighter's cockpit and make test runs, taxiing it back and forth on the runway. This Johnson had done many times, all without incident.

On September 20, the day shift had performed maintenance on the F-86F Sabre, no. 52.5039. Their work proved faulty and had to be corrected by Johnson and the rest of the night shift crew.

After completing the necessary work, the crew was expected to run a functional check on the repairs. Johnson

The jet-powered T-38A Talon is an advanced trainer. Here the two cockpits are visible. The instructor sits in the rear cockpit.

Piper Cub, similar to the one George Johnson used as a student pilot. Piper Cubs saw service in the US military during World War II and the Korean War. Light, affordable, and easy to fly, it is arguably the most famous general aviation trainer ever built.

conducted the check and, satisfied, he grabbed his headset and microphone, climbed into the Sabre's cockpit, and started the engine to finish the tests. Protocol called for him to taxi the jet to a spur just off the main runway (called a run-up area) where the engine tests were conducted and monitored.

Johnson called the control tower, requested and received permission to taxi to the run-up area. With the engine check completed, Johnson called the control tower again and asked for permission to use the runway for a high-speed taxi test, a standard check on work done to the brakes or nosewheel.

After receiving permission, Johnson guided the fighter onto the runway and accelerated. When he reached 120 miles per hour, he felt the nose getting light, and a few seconds later he felt the Sabre getting light on the main gear. Johnson later said, "I never had a conscious intention to fly that airplane. . . . I just didn't think I had enough room to stop." As he neared the end of the runway, he focused on maintaining climb speed. Once he was sure of his climb, he retracted the landing gear. At 10:34 p.m., September 20, 1956, Airman First Class George R. Johnson, now a Sabre fighter pilot, was airborne.

Though Johnson was calmly cruising through the air northwest of the airfield, things were anything but calm on the ground. In the control tower that night, Airman First Class Theodore Davis Jr. had given Johnson permission to run the tests that had now gone seriously awry. After failing to reestablish contact with Johnson, he notified Officer of the Day Captain Robert McCormick, who in turn notified base commander Colonel Jerry Page and Fire Chief Edward Anderson.

By the time Captain McCormick had reached the control tower, Davis had succeeded in establishing contact with Johnson who, still calm, requested instructions on what he should do. He was told to go into a holding pattern a few miles away and to stay away from any residential area while they figured out how to get him down safely.

Because Johnson was flying without a parachute, he would have to land the plane. Sabre pilot Second Lieutenant George Madison was Johnson's supervisor and,

(Continued on page 60)

CHARLES E. "CHUCK" YEAGER, BRIGADIER GENERAL, USAF (RET.)

Charles Elwood "Chuck" Yeager fought in World War II, where he became an ace, downing eleven planes; later, he served as a wing commander in the Vietnam War. He has been called "the fastest man alive" because he was the first man to break the sound barrier in an airplane on October 14, 1947, in the Bell X-1. What follows is an excerpt from his autobiography, *Yeager*, which eloquently describes the lure, sensation, and pure *fun* of flying.

You're whipping through a desert canyon at three hundred miles an hour, your belly just barely scraping the rocks and sagebrush. . . . It's a crystal-clear morning on the desert of western Nevada, and the joy of flying—the sense of speed and exhilaration twenty feet above the deck— makes you so damned happy that you want to shout for joy. . . . You feel so lucky, so blessed to be a fighter pilot.

TOP: Chuck Yeager standing beside the Bell X-1 "Glamourous Glennis," named after his wife. Yeager was a World War II ace, with eleven and a half victories. After the war he became a test pilot. On October 14, 1947, he made history when he broke the sound barrier in the X-1, earning him the nickname "the fastest man on earth."

OPPOSITE: A Bell X-1 similar to the one flown by Chuck Yeager when he broke the sound barrier in 1947. Here it is mounted on a B-29 Superfortress modified to carry the X-1. Once the B-29 reached mission altitude, the X-1 pilot would open a hatch in the B-29's fuselage, reach over and open the hatch in the X-1, and then crawl from the B-29 into the cockpit of the X-1.

(Continued from page 57)

at Johnson's suggestion, 2nd Lieutenant Madison flew up in another F-86 to guide Johnson in. Fortunately, there was no turbulence that night and 2nd Lieutenant Madison was able to escort Johnson safely down. Johnson was told that, when the wheels of his Sabre's landing gear touched the runway, he was to cut power and let the fighter coast into the crash barrier at the end of the runway. When Sabre no. 52.5039 stopped, Johnson's aerial adventure came to a halt, one hour and two minutes after it began.

The next day, Colonel Page visited Johnson in his hospital room where he had been taken for tests. After praising the airman for his extraordinary flying skill and calm demeanor throughout the flight, the base commander broke the bad news. Johnson was going to be court-martialed. If he showed any leniency, Colonel Page said, "I would have half of my mechanics trying the same damn fool stunt tomorrow."

Johnson was charged on three counts: stealing an F-86F, damaging it, and flying the Sabre without proper flying orders or clearance. The trial lasted one day. The theft charge was dropped, and Johnson pleaded guilty to the lesser charge of wrongful appropriation. He was found guilty on the second charge. The third charge was dropped as well, on the grounds that only pilots were subject to that regulation.

Though not given a dishonorable discharge, he was busted in rank to Airman Basic (Private), had his pay docked until the repair bill was paid, and sentenced to six months in jail. He was released after five months on good behavior. He served another two years in the Air Force and was honorably discharged with the rank of Airman Second Class.

Of that night adventure, Johnson later recalled, "It was kind of a dumb thing to do, but I got away with it. Had a guardian angel on my shoulder that night."

LEFT: The F-86 Sabre became famous as the symbol of US military aviation during the Korean War. On May 18, 1953, aviation pioneer Jacqueline Cochran became the first woman to break the sound barrier flying a modified F-86 Sabre.

OPPOSITE: A Republic F-86 Sabre, similar to the one George R. Johnson flew.

JOLLEY ROGER

Pilot·Cliff Jolley

SPECIAL THANKS:
TOM AND DAN FRIEDKIN
HORSEMEN FLIGHT TEAM
HERITAGE FLIGHT   USAF

6 THE ORIGINAL TOPGUNS

World War I was the first conflict in which pilots dueled in aerial combat. It saw the debut of the term "ace" to describe a pilot who scored a minimum of five aerial victories (more on that in Chapter 10). Any count of aces in the war (or any war in which aces were recognized) is at best an estimate, because it wasn't always possible to determine who downed an enemy plane, to sort out overlapping claims (often resulting in shared "half" credits), or to confirm if a plane was just damaged or shot down. According to a US Air War College study, there were a total of 1,305 aces in World War I from twelve countries. Here are some stories of the exceptional knights of the air from the Great War.

FRENCH ACES

René Fonck was France's top ace in World War I, with a confirmed seventy-five victories (and another sixty-seven listed as "probable"—a word that appears often in any discussion of aces). He was also the top Allied ace, or "ace of aces," in both World Wars I and II.

Fonck was such a deadly shooter that he often needed no more than a single burst of five rounds from his machine gun to down an enemy airplane. After the war, he wrote his autobiography, became a member of the French parliament, and, in 1926, attempted to make a solo transatlantic flight. Setting off from France for North America (a more difficult feat than the other direction, as he was flying into the wind), his landing gear collapsed during takeoff, ending his attempt before it began. Seven months later, in May 1927, Charles Lindbergh became the first to successfully make a transatlantic flight, from New York City to Paris.

GREAT BRITAIN AND THE COMMONWEALTH ACES

Great Britain didn't lionize aces to the extent that its allies or Germany did. Its government and military believed that doing so would slight the heroism of pilots flying other types of aircraft. Still, Britain and the Commonwealth (in this case Canada, South Africa, and Australia) did produce a number of aces lauded as heroes by their countrymen.

William "Billy" Bishop, with seventy-two victories, was Canada's top ace in World War I. When war broke out, he enlisted in the Royal Canadian Army. A crack shot, he transferred to the Royal Flying Corps in 1915, received his wings in 1916, and was assigned to night patrol over London against German zeppelin attack.

Itching for combat action, Bishop wrangled a transfer to France, where he joined 60 Squadron. Allowed to conduct

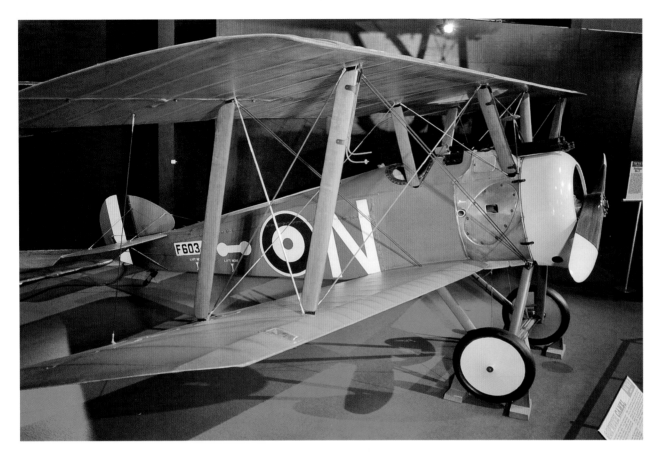

ABOVE: Georges Guynemer was one of France's top aces, with fifty-four victories. Like so many other aces of World War I, he did not survive the conflict, killed in action in September 1917.

LEFT: The Sopwith Camel arrived late in the war in June 1917. Nevertheless, it became the most famous British fighter in the war, probably because Captain Arthur Roy Brown of the Royal Canadian Air Force was flying a Camel when he allegedly shot down the Red Baron, Manfred von Richthofen, an action later credited to ground fire.

"lone wolf" sorties in addition to squadron sweeps, Bishop's kill total rapidly mounted. When he first made ace, his crew chief painted the nose of his fighter blue, then regarded as the mark of an ace. Not long after, his German adversaries dubbed him "Hell's Handmaiden," and one Jasta (German fighter squadron) put a bounty on him.

In 1918, by far Canada's ace of aces, the Canadian government became concerned over the potential negative impact on morale should he be shot down and killed (a legitimate concern as the mortality rate among pilots was

enormously high). Because of this, it grounded Bishop and sent him back to Canada, where he was given a senior position on the Canadian General Staff.

During World War II, Bishop served as an air marshal in the Royal Canadian Air Force, responsible for recruitment. He was so successful at it that volunteers had to be turned away.

Royal Flying Corps Captain Albert Ball was Britain's first ace to be celebrated as such. Captain Ball earned his wings in 1916 and, like so many other pilots who later

ABOVE: Harvard alumnus and lawyer Norman Prince was a founder of what became the Lafayette Escadrille squadron of American aviators fighting for the Allies prior to America's entry in World War I. He became an ace with five confirmed victories. He died in a landing accident on October 15, 1916, and was posthumously awarded France's Legion of Honor, its highest decoration.

RIGHT: Canadian fighter pilot Captain Albert Ball sits in the cockpit of his Royal Flying Corps S.E.5. Described as the "Spitfire of World War I" because of its combination of speed and maneuverability, it played an important role in establishing Allied Air superiority in 1917. Note the Lewis gun mounted on the top wing, indicating that it predates synchronized firing through the propeller.

became aces, initially flew reconnaissance missions. In May of that year, he was transferred to No. 11 Squadron; shortly thereafter he began downing enemy planes.

Unlike many of his peers, Captain Ball was a religious man with strong principles; he did not hate, nor did he enjoy killing, enemy pilots. His many letters to his parents were preserved and later published. This excerpt is typical: "I only scrap because it is my duty, but I do not think bad about the Hun. . . . Nothing makes me feel more rotten than to see them go down, but you see it is either them or me, so I must do my best to make it a case of them."

By May 1917, he had racked up a tally of forty-three confirmed and twenty-five unconfirmed victories. (The reason Allied pilots had so many unconfirmed kills in this war was that gun cameras to record shootdowns were not installed in aircraft until World War II. Most aerial combat took place over German-held territory, thus making it harder for Allied pilots to confirm whether or not a plane had been shot down.) His last flight occurred on May 7, 1917. Captain Ball engaged in a dogfight against Lothar von Richthofen, brother to the Red Baron, and succeeded in shooting him down for victory number forty-four (Lothar survived). Captain Ball in turn was either shot down by the Red Baron himself, by another pilot from his Jasta, or he became disoriented in the heavy overcast. Regardless of the cause, Captain Ball's fighter crashed in the ground near Douai in northern France and he was killed. He was twenty years old.

Captain Ball was posthumously awarded the Victoria Cross, Britain's highest decoration for valor. It was a devastating blow to civilian morale. In an effort to help restore it, a biography was quickly published that contained many of his letters to his parents. In his introduction to the book, Prime Minister David Lloyd George wrote:

> I am sure nobody can read these letters without feeling that it is men like Captain Ball who are the true soldiers of British democracy. It is their spirit of fearless activity for the right, in their daily work, which will lead us through victory into a new world in which tyranny and oppression will have no part.

UNITED STATES ACES

The United States officially entered the war on April 6, 1917—a "Johnny-come-lately" as far as the many Americans already in France were concerned. And when it did, Naval Aviation was a nonfactor in the war. Long before their country became an official combatant on the side of the Allies, dozens, then hundreds, of Americans crossed the Atlantic Ocean to help the British and French against Germany, Austria-Hungary, and the Ottoman Empire. Most did so in logistics fields or, like author Ernest Hemingway, as ambulance drivers. Among that group was a collection of young men, almost all of them Ivy Leaguers and drawn from wealthy families, who fought over the skies of Europe in a squadron known as the Lafayette Escadrille.

The brainchild of William Thaw and Norman Prince, whose families were among the hundred richest in America, they convinced the French government to authorize a squadron of American pilots who would fight for them. Recognizing its propaganda value in helping to sway isolationist American public opinion to the Allied cause, the French agreed. Squadron 124, as it was designated, received the name Escadrille Américaine. A German diplomatic protest that the name violated US neutrality forced a name change in honor of the Marquis de Lafayette, the French nobleman who fought in the American army during the Revolutionary War.

Activated on April 20, 1916, it was disbanded almost two years later on February 18, 1918, when its members were incorporated into the US Army Air Service. By then, they had become what former Air Force Chief of Staff General T. Michael Moseley called "the founding fathers of American combat aviation." Their devil-may-care attitude and joie de vivre established the fighter pilot ethos that continues to this day. A number of the squadron's pilots were aces by the time they joined the air service, and the greatest of them was Gervais Raoul Lufbery, known as "Luf."

The son of an American father and French mother, Lufbery was born in France and spent most of his life there, though he always considered himself first and foremost American. His skill as a mechanic impressed French aviator

LEFT: Gervais Raoul Lufbery was one of America's great aces in the war. As with so many of his contemporaries, he did not survive it.

OPPOSITE: A group of American pilots, including founders Chapman and Thaw, of the Lafayette Escadrille at their aerodrome in France. From left to right: Victor Chapman, Elliott Cowdin, William Thaw, Norman Prince, Kiffin Rockwell, Bert Hall, Lieutenant Alfred De Laage De Meux, James Rogers McConnell, and Captain Georges Thenault.

Marc Pourpe, who hired him to maintain his airplane during his prewar barnstorming exploits. When war broke out, Pourpe joined the French Air Force and Lufbery the Foreign Legion as an infantryman. When Pourpe was killed in action, Lufbery transferred to the air force in order to learn how to fly and avenge the death of his friend.

What he lacked in natural flying skills, he more than made up for in meticulous persistence. The top-wing-mounted Lewis gun was notorious for jamming. Before each mission, Lufbery would hand inspect each bullet for defects and polish them to insure smooth firing. He also did his own maintenance on his airplane. Fellow pilot Edward Hinckle said, "Anyone would rather have a secondhand Lufbery machine than a new one anytime." When he went into combat, he held his fire until he was in point-blank range. By the time the Lafayette Escadrille was disbanded, Lufbery was an ace three times over and was credited with creating the defensive maneuver known as the Lufbery circle, in which the squadron forms a large circle for mutual defense.

Transferred to the 94th Aero Squadron, which became famous as the "Hat in the Ring" squadron, one of the new pilots he took under his wing to mentor in the deadly art of aerial combat was Eddie Rickenbacker. Lufbery took Rickenbacker on his first sortie—a reconnaissance mission as the machine guns allotted to them had yet to arrive. Squadron mate Bill Jackson recalled, "When they came back, he asked Rickenbacker if he'd seen any Germans, and Rickenbacker said, 'No.' So Lufbery told him to look at his plane and there were four holes in it." Lufbery then told him of a German squadron that had flown past well below them and pointed to other battle damage Rickenbacker's plane had suffered. After the war, Rickenbacker acknowledged, "Everything I learned, I learned from Lufbery."

On May 19, 1918, Lufbery was flying a different plane, as his was unavailable. He attacked an enemy observation plane flying near the American airfield. Accounts vary as to what happened next.

At first it was reported that his plane had burst into flames and Lufbery had leapt out, perhaps in an attempt to dive into the nearby Moselle River. Later accounts state that he had loosened his seatbelt in order to clear his jammed

Lewis gun, so that, when his plane flipped over on its back, he fell out. As pilots did not wear parachutes back then, it was a death plunge. Lufbery was buried with full military honors, aged thirty-three.

Lufbery's protégé, US Army Air Corps Captain Edward Vernon "Eddie" Rickenbacker, was America's ace of aces in the war. He logged twenty-six confirmed kills, though he almost wound up in a jail cell instead of a fighter cockpit when he tried to enlist.

RIGHT: Captain Eddie Rickenbacker wearing his Medal of Honor.

BELOW: With twenty-six aerial victories, Captain Eddie Rickenbacker was America's ace of aces in World War I.

SPAD S.XIII

The SPAD S.XIII was the last in the line of successful biplane fighters designed by the French manufacturer Société Pour L'Aviation et ses Dérivés (SPAD). One of the most-produced warplanes in World War I, almost 8,500 examples of the S.XIII model were built, with nearly 900 going to the United States Army Air Service.

The SPAD S.XIII mounted two synchronized Vickers machine guns above the engine and was a powerful, rugged, high-performance fighter with excellent diving characteristics. It consistently outperformed top German fighters. Seventeen American squadrons flew it. Captain Eddie Rickenbacker scored twenty of his twenty-six air victories in an S.XIII.

On September 25, 1918, he was flying a voluntary, solo patrol for the northern French city of Billy when he spotted five Fokker fighters escorting two Halberstadt photoreconnaissance planes. Despite the odds, Rickenbacker attacked, downing one fighter and one photorecon plane, forcing the rest to return to base. For this action, he earned the Medal of Honor.

This SPAD S.XIII sports the livery of the 94th Aero Squadron, known as the "Hat in the Ring" squadron, of which Captain Eddie Rickenbacker was a member.

He was born in Columbus, Ohio, to Swiss-German immigrant parents. When the United States entered the war on the side of the Allies in 1917, anti-German sentiment had reached hysterical levels—anyone or anything that had a German (or German-sounding) name was suspect. Even food products were affected; one of the most famous examples of this was the renaming of sauerkraut as "liberty cabbage."

Despite his prewar fame as a race car driver (he competed four times in the Indianapolis 500, among other races), he found it prudent to change his Swiss-German name, Richenbacher, to the more English-sounding Rickenbacker. It was a cosmetic move that didn't help much: when he attempted to enlist, the recruiters interrogated him, suspecting that he was a German spy.

Rickenbacker was posted to the 94th Aero Squadron, which became famous as the "Hat in the Ring" squadron. He shot down his first plane on April 29, 1918. A month later almost to the day, he downed his fifth warplane and became an ace; he received the French Croix de Guerre in recognition of that achievement. Rickenbacker was ultimately awarded the Medal of Honor and an unprecedented ten Distinguished Service Crosses, among other decorations.

Though he had many brushes with death on the racetrack and in the cockpit, it was a flight as a passenger

in a B-17 Flying Fortress bomber during World War II that came closest to killing him.

In 1942, he was sent on an inspection tour of Pacific air bases, as a special observer for the War Department and to deliver a secret message to theater commander General Douglas MacArthur in Australia. In October, after departing Hawaii, the B-17 lost its navigation fix. Forced to ditch in the Pacific Ocean, Rickenbacker and the crew all safely got into life rafts—with only four oranges between them for food. Their epic of survival lasted twenty-one days before the raft was spotted by a Navy observation plane and everyone was rescued.

Rickenbacker later became an executive of Eastern Air Lines. He died in Switzerland in 1973, aged eighty-two.

GERMAN ACES

As good as Oswald Boelcke was in combat—and he was *very* good, credited with forty kills—he was an even better teacher and tactician. Having received Germany's highest decoration, the Pour le Mérite, he was also lauded as the founder of the German fighter air force and the "Father of Air Fighting Tactics." His career was impressive, especially considering the fact that, when he was killed in action in October 1916, he was only twenty-five years old!

His companion in the air, Max Immelmann, was a skilled tactician as well. He created a half-roll on top of a half-loop maneuver, dubbed the "Immelmann Turn," which is still used today.

Immelmann was the first aviator to be awarded the Pour le Mérite (Boelcke received his a few minutes later in the same ceremony), leading the decoration to be nicknamed the "Blue Max." Like his pilot comrade, Immelmann did not survive the war: he was killed in action in June 1916, aged twenty-five.

It would take an extraordinary pilot to overshadow Boelcke and Immelman in the eyes of Germans, and the one who did it was Boelcke's protégé, Baron Manfred Albrecht Freiherr von Richthofen, the Red Baron. He was Germany's ace of aces, the greatest ace of World War I—as well as

ABOVE: Oswald Boelcke was one of the early heroic aces for Germany. His death in October 1916 devastated German morale.

LEFT: One of the inflatable rafts used by Eddie Rickenbacker and the B-17 crew after they crash-landed in the Pacific Ocean. They drifted for three weeks before being rescued.

Snoopy's arch-nemesis. Boelcke's deadliest student, von Richthofen logged eighty confirmed aerial victories, the most in the war.

The aristocratic von Richthofen loved hunting and horses, but he was not a natural pilot. Prompted by Boelcke, it was only with difficulty that he learned how to fly. His instructor only allowed him to solo after his twenty-fifth flight, considerably longer than his fellow students, and the result was less than stellar. Alone in the cockpit for the first time, von Richthofen crashed his airplane while attempting to land. There's an axiom among pilots that any good landing is one you can walk away from, and fortunately for him (though not his future victims) he was able to do so.

In August 1916, Boelcke selected von Richthofen to be a member of a squadron he was forming, Jagdstaffel 2 (shortened to Jasta 2), where von Richthofen would make his reputation. Though he had previously shot down a handful of enemy planes, those victories were unconfirmed. It was not until September 17, 1916, that he recorded his first confirmed victory, shooting down a Royal Flying Corps F.E.2 observation plane over Cambrai, France. He commemorated that victory by ordering a silver cup inscribed with the date of victory and type of plane. He continued the practice, stopping at his sixtieth victory when supplies of silver had dried up due to Allied blockade.

He became the commander of Jasta 11 in January 1917. Soon after, he decided to have his plane, an Albatros D.III biplane, painted bright red. His squadron mates soon followed suit, and thus was born the legend of the Red Baron and his Flying Circus, an enormous propaganda coup for Germany.

Von Richthofen did not begin flying the Fokker Dr. 1 triplane until July 1917, and only scored nineteen of his eighty victories with it. Still, his bright red Fokker Dr. 1 with its distinctive three wings is the fighter most associated with him.

Like Boelcke, Immelmann, and so many other top fighter pilots on both sides, von Richthofen did not survive the war. Canadian pilot Captain Arthur "Roy" Brown is credited with shooting down and killing the Red Baron on April 21, 1918, in a dogfight over a unit of Australian soldiers, for which he was decorated. Subsequently,

sufficient evidence was gathered to suggest that von Richthofen was killed by ground fire.

His death was a devastating blow to German morale. His body was treated with respect by his enemies, who gave him a funeral with full military honors and buried him in the village of Bertangles in northern France. It would have been unusual for a hero of von Richthofen's stature to remain buried in an obscure village in a foreign country and, as it turned out, it took several decades before von Richthofen's remains could finally rest in peace.

FOKKER DR. 1 DREIDECKER

Though it arrived late in the war (September 1917) and few were built (only 320), the Fokker Dr. 1 Dreidecker triplane is arguably the most famous warplane of World War I. Without question, though, thanks to Baron Manfred von Richthofen, it is the most recognizable plane from the war. With its distinctive three wings (*drei decker*) and scarlet-red color scheme, von Richthofen flew the fighter into history.

His squadron was flying the Albatros D.III when two preproduction models, labeled F.1, were delivered to him. Von Richthofen took one of them up; within two days, he'd shot down his sixtieth and sixty-first aircraft. In his after-action report, he stated that the Fokker triplane was superior to Britain's Sopwith (the Fokker triplane was intended to be Germany's answer to the British fighter) and recommended that fighter squadrons be equipped with the new Fokkers as quickly as possible.

Highly maneuverable and regarded fondly by pilots, it was also a temperamental aircraft and prone to accidents during landing. When von Richthofen was shot down and killed behind Canadian army lines, his Fokker Dr. 1 was stripped to the bone by souvenir hunters.

With its three wings, the Fokker Dr. 1 triplane was already the most distinctive fighter in World War I. When Baron Manfred von Richthofen decided to paint it a brilliant red, it became even more recognizable—and feared.

BELOW: Baron Manfred von Richthofen was Germany's ace of aces in World War I, with eighty victories. His death in 1918 was cause for national mourning.

RIGHT: Australian soldiers give a rifle salute at the graveside of Baron von Richthofen at the conclusion of his funeral with full military honors in France.

In the early 1920s, the French government exhumed his body and reburied it with other German war dead in a special military cemetery in nearby Fricourt. The von Richthofen family petitioned the French government in 1923 to repatriate his remains to Germany, where they planned to bury him beside his father and brother Lothar (also an ace, who died in a postwar accident). Upon being granted permission, the German government stepped in and asked instead that von Richthofen be buried in Berlin at a cemetery containing many of its military heroes and important citizens. The family agreed to this change of plans. For the third time, in a state funeral ceremony, his body was laid to rest.

After World War II, Nazi Germany was divided into four zones of military occupation by the victorious Allies, as was Berlin, its capital. The cemetery where von Richthofen was buried was in the Soviet zone, later a part of Communist East Germany, and his grave and its marker were repeatedly vandalized during the Cold War. In 1975, for the second time in family history, von Richthofen's descendants petitioned for his body to be exhumed and buried in the family plot located in Wiesbaden, in what was then democratic West Germany. Von Richthofen was buried, for the fourth time, in the family plot where he will, hopefully, finally, rest in peace.

7 /// THE HIGH-FLYING HEROES OF WORLD WAR II

24 October 1944; 0750 hours
USS Essex

The ear-grating order came through the loudspeaker in the pilots' ready room. The pilots of Air Group 15 were ordered to man their planes, with one exception: "All except air group commander. He is not, repeat not, to go."

Commander David McCampbell, Air Group 15's commander, air group (CAG), slumped in his chair as the rest of the pilots filed out of the ready room and up to their F6F Hellcat fighters warming up on the flight deck above. Instead of leading his men into battle, the Navy's top ace, with twenty-one Japanese kills, would have to cool his heels, a victim of his admiral's ire.

Three days earlier, Commander McCampbell had flown a personal sweep mission. Rear Admiral Frederick Sherman, Commander, Task Group 38.3, had gotten wind of his little solo target-of-opportunity "joyride" and gave the truant CAG a dressing-down. Now Commander McCampbell found himself suffering the worst punishment a fighter pilot could receive: sitting out a battle.

Just as he was resigning himself to his fate, the ready room's loudspeaker squawked, "Now hear this . . . air group commander is to fly, repeat, affirmative, air group

commander is to go." Commander McCampbell jumped up, grabbed his gear, and dashed up to the flight deck. When he reached his fighter, his crew chief told him that his Hellcat's gas tanks were only half full. Having no choice but to risk running out of gas in the middle of a dogfight, he jumped into his plane and led the last group of seven fighters on an intercept course against what was described as a large group of bogeys heading toward the fleet.

Twenty-two miles out, Commander McCampbell saw them: a sky filled with more than sixty Japanese warplanes heading toward the fleet. He immediately radioed for assistance and was told none was available—all the planes from the task force were attacking other targets. Though vastly outnumbered, Commander McCampbell ordered his men to charge their machine guns. They were going in. He ordered five of his pilots to attack the Japanese bombers flying below, while he and his wingman, Lieutenant Roy Rushing, attacked the large escort of Zeros and Oscars (army Nakajima fighters) flying high.

Commander McCampbell and Lieutenant Rushing took position above the enemy fighters, who in response had formed a defensive Lufbery circle formation, ready to pounce the moment an opening presented itself. Whenever a pair of fighters tried to make a break for it, or when one broke formation and became a straggler, the two US Navy pilots pounced and began racking up kills. Lieutenant Rushing became an ace, logging six confirmed kills and two probables; Commander McCampbell shot down nine confirmed. After an hour and a half of the deadly aerial *pas de deux*, he realized that he was flying a plane with only half a load of gas. Instead of adding to his score, Commander McCampbell broke off action and, together with Lieutenant Rushing, began a nerve-wracking flight back to the fleet.

As he neared the *Essex*, he was told to circle the carrier, as her flight deck was full of planes from another strike. After checking his gas gauge, he said he'd have to ditch, as his tanks were almost empty. He was ordered to the carrier *Langley*, where enough planes were cleared from the flight deck for him to land. When he did, the flight deck crew had to push the plane away: the gas tanks were bone dry.

When he finally returned to the *Essex*, he was ordered to report to Admiral Sherman. He glared at Commander McCampbell and demanded to know why the pilot had disobeyed a direct order. Commander McCampbell explained that he'd gotten an order from the air officer and he assumed that the officer had received permission from the admiral. "He did not," Admiral Sherman growled. After being told to never "let it happen again," Commander McCampbell was dismissed.

No doubt it was the downing of nine enemy planes in one engagement that saved his skin. Because, instead of being court-martialed for taking off from the *Essex*'s flight deck that day, Commander David McCampbell was awarded the Medal of Honor; and Lieutenant Roy Rushing was awarded the Navy's second highest decoration for valor, the Navy Cross.

(Continued on page 80)

Commander David McCampbell, the US Navy's top ace in World War II. Painted on the fuselage below the cowling of his F6F Hellcat are miniature flags of the Japanese navy indicating the planes he has shot down.

SUPERMARINE SPITFIRE

The Spitfire is the most famous British warbird of World War II. With its sleek fuselage and distinctive elliptical wings, it is one of the most graceful and beautiful aircraft ever built.

The Spitfire was one of the first all-metal, low-wing, retractable-undercarriage, enclosed-canopy monoplane fighters. Remarkably, it remained in production for eleven years, from 1938 to 1949.

The Spitfire achieved enduring fame as one of the fighters flown by "the few"—the pilots that saved Great Britain during the Battle of Britain in 1940. While the United States was neutral (prior to Pearl Harbor), a handful of American pilots fought for England as members of the Eagle Squadron. One of them was Pilot Officer John Gillespie Magee Jr., who served in the Royal Canadian Air Force. On August 8, 1941, his experience while flying a Spitfire Mk I inspired him to write a sonnet, *High Flight*, which became the official poem of the Royal Canadian Air Force and the Royal Air Force. First-year cadets at the United States Air Force Academy are required to memorize it. Tragically, Magee died in a midair collision some months after he wrote the poem.

High Flight

Oh! I have slipped the surly bonds of Earth
And danced the skies on laughter-silvered wings:
Sunward I've climbed, and joined the tumbling mirth
Of sun-split clouds,—and done a hundred things
You have not dreamed of—wheeled and soared and swung
High in the sunlit silence. Hov'ring there,
I've chased the shouting wind along, and flung
My eager craft through footless halls of air . . .

Up, up the long, delirious, burning blue
I've topped the wind-swept heights with easy grace
Where never lark nor even eagle flew—
And, while with silent lifting mind I've trod
The high untrespassed sanctity of space,
Put out my hand, and touched the face of God.

LOCKHEED
P-38 LIGHTNING

With its distinctive twin-boom configuration, the P-38 Lightning was the most recognizable warplane of World War II. For that reason, the P-38 was the only Allied aircraft authorized to fly over the Normandy landing beaches during D-Day on June 6, 1944, even though all the Allied aircraft had their fuselages and wings painted with identifying alternating black and white stripes. A radical and innovative departure in design, the Lightning was one of the truly great fighter planes ever built. The top two American aces in the war, Major Richard Bong and Major Thomas McGuire, would rack up their respective forty and thirty-eight victories in Lightnings.

The Lightning participated in one of the most important intercept missions of the war. American intelligence had intercepted the flight plans of Japanese Admiral Yamamoto Isoroku, the mastermind of the attack on Pearl Harbor on December 7, 1941, that plunged America into war. On April 18, 1943, sixteen P-38G Lightnings, carrying external wing tanks to extend their range, took off from their base on the Southwest Pacific island of Guadalcanal. They flew 435 miles at no more than 50 feet above the water. They arrived at Bougainville island just as Admiral Yamamoto's plane was about to land. Lieutenant Rex T. Barber was credited with shooting down Yamamoto's plane and, in recognition, he received the Navy Cross, a noteworthy gesture of gratitude by the US Navy, as Lieutenant Barber was a US Army Air Force officer.

ABOVE: With its twin-boomed tail, the Lockheed Lightning was the most easily identifiable aircraft in World War II. Because of that, it was the only Allied fighter allowed to fly over Allied lines during Operation Overlord, the invasion of Normandy.

OPPOSITE: This closeup of the nose of the Lightning reveals why it was so deadly in combat. Because its engines flanked the cockpit, the combination of machine guns and cannon could be concentrated in the nose, giving it tremendous firepower.

(Continued from page 76)

THE GOLDEN AGE OF ACES

If ever there was a Golden Age for aces, it was World War II. A study by the Air War College estimated that the conflict produced more than 4,000 aces from twenty-four countries. The United States topped the list with 1,283. At the other end, with one ace each, are Yugoslavia, Iceland, Greece, and the Netherlands. The list also includes two women, both from the Soviet Union: Lydia Litvyak (twelve victories) and Yekaterina Budanova (six). As with the aces of World War I, the numbers credited to the aces mentioned here are, at best, estimates; in some cases, official records vary widely with long-accepted claims. Planes listed as probably shot down could very well be actual kills, but in the life-and-death melee that is an aerial dogfight, if a pilot decides to follow a damaged enemy plane down, he risks getting shot down himself.

World War II's ace of aces was Germany's Erich Hartmann, with 352 victories, followed by his countryman, Gerhard Barkhorn (301). Japan's top ace was Tetsuzo Iwamoto (eighty). The Soviet Union's top ace (and top Allied ace) was Ivan Kozledub (sixty-six—or sixty-eight, if you include the two American P-51 Mustangs he shot down because they mistakenly attacked him). The top ace from the British Commonwealth was South African Marmaduke Thomas St. John Pattle (forty), and from Great Britain, James Edgar "Johnnie" Johnson (thirty-eight).

America's ace of aces was the Army Air Force's Richard Bong (forty), followed by his AAF rival in the southwest Pacific and Philippines, Tommy McGuire (thirty-eight). David McCampbell was the Navy's top ace (thirty-four). Gregory "Pappy" Boyington was the Marine Corps's top ace, if you allow his tally to include the six Japanese planes he shot down while serving as a mercenary for the Nationalist Chinese in the American Volunteer Group (better known as the "Flying Tigers")

(twenty-eight); otherwise, he would come in second behind Joseph Foss (twenty-six). Like McCampbell, Bong, McGuire, Boyington, and Foss also received the Medal of Honor.

A variety of factors contributed to the disparity of victory tallies between the top German and Allied aces. These included aircraft superiority (particularly in the early part of the war), the theater of operations (Hartmann and other top German aces fought in the Eastern Front against less-experienced pilots who were flying inferior aircraft), and, perhaps most importantly, policy.

With one exception, the major Allies, particularly the United States, had a rotation policy that regularly reassigned its pilots, usually sending them back to the States to conduct war bond drives, give morale-boosting speeches, and pass on lessons learned to pilots undergoing training. The exception was the Soviet Union; as with Germany, pilots from the USSR flew and fought until they were either too severely wounded to fly or they were killed.

LEFT: A Japanese kamikaze smashes into the flight deck of the USS *Essex* during operations off the Philippines in November 1944. Despite suffering extensive damage, the *Essex* was repaired and had a long, distinguished career before being decommissioned in 1969.

RIGHT: America's ace of aces in World War II was Army Air Force Major Richard Bong, with forty victories. All of his victories were achieved in the Pacific Theater of Operations and in the twin-boomed P-38 Lightning.

MESSERSCHMITT BF-109

The fighter flown by most of Germany's top aces was the Messerschmitt Bf-109. It was one of the few planes in the war to serve as a frontline fighter from start to finish. There had been initial suspicions that its innovative, advanced design made it too risky to fly. When World War II ended in 1945, however, the Bf-109 was the standard against which all other World War II fighters would be judged.

The Bf-109 served the Luftwaffe in almost every capacity possible for an aircraft, including interceptor, fighter-bomber, night-fighter, photoreconnaissance, escort, and ground attack. With more than 30,000 built, more 109s were produced and in more variants than any other aircraft then and today.

Germany's ace of aces Erich Hartmann flew the Bf-109. To his countrymen, he was the "Blond Knight of Germany," but the Soviets saw him as the "Black Devil of the Ukraine," and their respect for him was such that they placed a 10,000-ruble bounty on him (at a time when a lieutenant in the Red Army received about 7,700 rubles per year). Hartmann flew with the Luftwaffe's most successful fighter wing, Jagdgeschwader 52, and earned one of Germany's highest decorations, the Knight's Cross of the Iron Cross with Oak Leaves, Swords, and Diamonds.

Hartmann's squadron was known as the "Sweetheart Squadron" for the distinctive bleeding heart pierced by an arrow painted on the Bf-109's fuselage. Hartmann further identified his airplane with the painting of a black tulip. Soviet pilots had such respect for Hartmann's ability that, instead of trying to collect the bounty, squadrons would fly away when they saw that black tulip on the fuselage. Hartmann erased the black tulip—and once again began racking up victories. Never shot down and never wounded, Hartmann survived the war and, after release from a Soviet prison camp in 1955, became a pilot in the West German air force.

A Messerschmitt Bf-109.

8 TOPGUN IN KOREA

Once again, the outbreak of war caught the United States unprepared for conflict. This time it was on the Korean Peninsula in June 1950. In the post-World War II demobilization and drawdown, the country's millions of active-duty personnel and weapons were drastically reduced. Where before the US military comprised millions of men and women in uniform, now there were just a few hundred thousand. And the once-mighty armada that had successfully waged a two-ocean war had for the most part been sold for scrap or to other countries, or mothballed. The Air Force, on whose wings the nuclear strike military strategy rested, was rendered null and void when President Harry S. Truman rejected deploying the nation's nuclear arsenal to stop Communist North Korea's invasion of democratic South Korea, fearing that such a move would escalate the local crisis into World War III, just five years after the second globe-spanning conflict had ended. Instead, the Korean War would be fought with conventional arms and, for the first time, under the banner of the newly formed United Nations.

OPPOSITE: The Republic F-86 Sabre was America's top jet fighter in the Korean War. Prior to that conflict, the military changed the World War II designation for fighters, "P" for "Pursuit," to "F" for "Fighter."

The air war over Korea was notable for two things. Both sides used World War II–era, piston-powered warplanes and modern jet fighters: North Korea's top-of-the-line fighter was the Soviet-made MiG-15, while American forces fielded a variety of slower straight-wing and faster swept-wing jet fighters. Of the thirty-eight American pilots who made ace during the war, only one, Lieutenant Guy P. Bordelon Jr., was from the Navy; he accomplished that feat flying a World War II–vintage F-4U Corsair.

Nicknamed "Lucky Pierre," the Ruston, Louisiana, native earned his wings in 1943 and was a flight instructor during the war. In 1952, he joined a squadron flying the night fighter variant of the Corsair. In addition to his status as the Navy's only ace in Korea, Lieutenant Bordelon's achievement had two other distinctions: he was the only night ace, and he was the last one to make ace flying only a piston-powered fighter.

Major John Bolt, USMC, was a member of Major "Pappy" Boyington's famous Black Sheep squadron in World War II, where he shot down six Japanese warplanes. In Korea, he was initially assigned to a fighter-bomber squadron and conducted a variety of air-to-ground missions. Wishing to transfer to a fighter squadron, he took advantage of an officer exchange program and got transferred to the Air Force's 39th Fighter Interceptor Squadron flying the F-86 Sabre. While flying under Air Force colors, he shot down six more planes, making him one of only nine pilots to become aces in both World War II and the Korean War. He was paired with Lieutenant Joseph McConnell, who would go on to become the Korean War's top ace with sixteen victories. Major Bolt later assumed command of Lieutenant McConnell's flight when the latter was ordered home following that sixteenth victory.

Major Bolt's fourth MiG victory was perhaps his most dangerous, but not due to the combat involved. The encounter was preceded by trickery and insubordination that could have wrecked his career and that of his commanding officer.

Though battles themselves are monuments to chaos, they are fought under a set of protocols known as the rules of engagement (ROE). These can be quite restrictive, as we will see in the chapter on the Vietnam War.

The Yalu River forms North Korea's northern border with Communist China. North Korean pilots flew missions from air bases located near the northern bank of the Yalu River. Allied pilots were forbidden to attack those bases, as they were in Chinese territory. This was actually a violation of China's ostensible status as a neutral (which China

further violated when it sent an army of "volunteers" south to help North Korea fight United Nations forces). Also, the pilots in the North Korean–flagged planes were actually from the Soviet Union, a violation of its status as a neutral. But because President Truman didn't want to escalate the war, he turned a diplomatic blind eye to those violations.

Major Bolt's squadron commander was Colonel George Ruddell, already an ace with five kills of his own. Colonel Ruddell wanted to add to his score. But in the summer of 1953, there were no more MiGs to be had, at least not south of the Yalu River.

One night, after a few rounds of drinks, Colonel Ruddell confessed to Major Bolt that he was willing to risk his career and cross the Yalu to shoot down another MiG. Major Bolt agreed to help.

The next day, together with a pair of pilots flying Sabres specially equipped with navigational aids designed to deceive USAF air controllers, they took off and headed north.

ABOVE: Lieutenant Guy Bordelon was the Navy's only ace in the Korean War. He named his F4U-5N Corsair fighter *Annie-Mo*, in which he shot down five enemy aircraft over Korea.

LEFT: The Mikoyan-Gurevich MiG-15 was North Korea's top fighter in the Korean War. Small, fast, and maneuverable, it would later serve as North Vietnam's top fighter in the Vietnam War.

OPPOSITE: The Chance-Vought F-4U Corsair, the top Marine Corps fighter in World War II, was pressed into service to fight in the Korean War. Its distinctive gullwing design provided clearance for its large propeller. Here a Corsair is making a successful landing on an aircraft carrier with its tail hook.

At the Yalu, Colonel Ruddell and Major Bolt switched their radios to a communications channel not monitored by the air controllers and turned off their identification, friend or foe (IFF) beacons and zipped across the Yalu into China. Meanwhile, the other two pilots turned on their masking devices, which caused air controllers monitoring their air space to believe that they were still tracking four Sabres.

Colonel Ruddell and Major Bolt flew to 44,000 feet and soon spotted a MiG fighter. Though Colonel Ruddell was supposed to be the one to shoot it down, Major Bolt turned out to have the better angle, and he took it. Down went the MiG.

Not wishing to push their luck, they recrossed the Yalu, linked up with their coconspirators, reset their radios and controls, and returned to base without incident. Once back, Major Bolt was ribbed mercilessly for "stealing" his colonel's MiG.

The first pilot credited with being an ace in the war was Major James Jabara, USAF, whose official tally of fifteen planes ranked him second overall with Captain Joe McConnell (sixteen).

Major Jabara got his fifth and sixth victories on May 20, 1951, under deadly tit-for-tat circumstances. The Soviet MiG-15 is a nimble fighter, more maneuverable than the Sabre, and with a higher ceiling. On May 20, two flights (eight planes) of Sabres ran into a large group of MiGs flying in an area running parallel south of the Yalu River (dubbed "MiG Alley" by the American pilots because of the many MiGs patrolling there). Major Jabara was involved in another pair of flights when he heard a call for help in his headset.

Prior to going into combat, pilots release their external gas tanks to free their planes of the extra weight and drag. Unfortunately for Major Jabara, when he yanked the release, only one of his two wing tanks separated. Despite being off balance and with degraded maneuverability, Jabara disobeyed protocol that called for him to break off and return to base. Instead, he attacked and soon shot down his fifth MiG, becoming an ace.

In that engagement, he got separated from his wingman, an extremely dangerous situation for him given his fighter's condition. Sure enough, Major Jabara soon found himself on the receiving end of MiG cannon and machine gun fire. The

OPPOSITE: Major James Jabara, USAF, the first ace in the Korean War.

RIGHT: The Soviet-made MiG-15 was North Korea's top fighter in the Korean War. One of the first swept-wing fighters, it easily outclassed the propeller-driven, straight-wing jet fighters used by the United Nations military forces in the early months of the war.

BELOW: For years, the Soviet Union claimed that the MiG-15s used by the North Korea Air Force were flown by North Korean pilots. Only after the fall of the Soviet Union did former Soviet pilots confirm that they were the pilots in the cockpits.

MiG pilot scored hits on Major Jabara's Sabre. With his fighter pouring smoke and losing power and altitude, he nonetheless managed to shoot down his adversary for his sixth kill.

But now it looked like he would be the one to pay for his recklessness, when five MiGs swept in for the kill. Despite horsing his Sabre into violent combat maneuvers, Major Jabara couldn't dodge all the enemy fire and once again his aircraft received hits that he recalled "sounded like a popcorn machine right in my cockpit." Two F-86 pilots saw his plight and flew in to the rescue. Major Jabara managed to fly his heavily damaged Sabre back to base where, despite his two victories, he received a chewing out from his squadron commander for disobeying protocol.

The top ace in the Korean War, Captain Joseph P. McConnell (sixteen victories), almost didn't qualify as a jet fighter pilot. A bomber navigator during World War II, when war broke out in Korea in 1950, Captain McConnell was

(continued on page 91)

F-86 SABRE

The swept-wing F-86 Sabre was manufactured by North American Aviation, builders of the P-51 Mustang. It was the US Air Force's last true dogfighting fighter, and first fighter capable of carrying nuclear weapons (the F-86H variant). Standard armament was six .50-caliber machine guns mounted on each side of its nose. Hardpoints on the wings enabled it to carry rockets or bombs, up to 5,000 pounds of ordnance. Operational from 1949 to 1956, more than 7,800 Sabres were built, in eight variants.

An F-86A flown by Major Richard Johnson broke the sound barrier and set a world speed record of 6,712 miles an hour on September 15, 1948.

The Sabre became operational just in time for use in the Korean War where it became the Air Force's preeminent fighter. Sabres entered the war in December 1950, when the 4th Fighter Interceptor Wing was deployed. On December 17, Lieutenant Colonel Bruce H. Hinton became the first Sabre pilot to shoot down an enemy plane. At war's end in 1953, Lieutenant Colonel Hinton had succeeded in only doubling his score.

Seven of the F-86 pilots in Korea were aces in World War II. They included Colonel Francis S. "Gabby" Gabreski, who was one of the Air Force's top aces in that war, with twenty-eight victories. He achieved his ace status in Korea with a unique gunsight. Dissatisfied with the one mounted on his Sabre, he had it removed after downing his first MiG. He then replaced it with a piece of chewing gum stuck on the windshield, using it to shoot down another five-and-a-half MiGs.

Pilots loved flying the Sabre. Brigadier General Charles "Chuck" Yeager shared that sentiment, saying, "I dearly loved the Sabre, almost as much as I enjoyed the P-51 Mustang from World War II days. It was a terrific plane to fly."

(continued from page 87)

OPPOSITE: Captain Joseph P. McConnell, USAF, the ace of aces in the Korean War in the cockpit of his F-86 Sabre, "Beauteous Butch II," based on his wife's nickname. His sixteen victories are indicated by the stars painted on his plane's fuselage.

RIGHT: Colonel Francis S. "Gabby" Gabreski was an ace in both World War II and the Korean War.

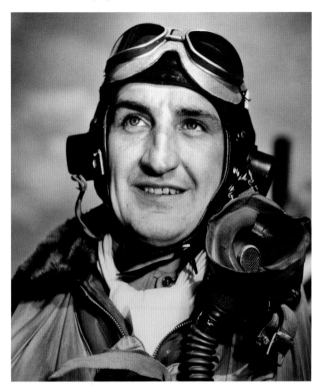

twenty-eight years old and considered too old to fly fighter jets. But he managed to convince his superiors and soon qualified to fly Sabres.

He didn't get deployed until late in the war, in August 1952, more than a year after armistice talks had begun. It took him another five months before he recorded his first kill on January 14, 1953. But from that point on, he was racking up kills. Within a month, he had shot down his fifth plane, reaching ace status. Three months after that, he achieved triple-ace status plus-1 by downing three MiGs on May 18. Upon receiving the news of Captain McConnell's

achievement, the Far East Air Force commander, Lieutenant General Glenn Barcus, was concerned that his top ace might be shot down and killed; he reportedly said, "I want that man on his way back home to the USA before you hear the period at the end of this sentence." Captain McConnell duly packed his bags and returned to the States.

He bagged his eighth victory on April 12, 1953. Strangely, the pilot he shot down, Soviet pilot Semen Alexeievich Fedorets, himself an ace with five victories, added to his score by shooting Captain McConnell down in what amounted to a tit-for-tat result of the engagement.

Of his attack, Fedorets later said, "I sharply broke to the right underneath the Sabre, getting out of the line of fire. The Sabre went forward, and ended up in front of me at my right."

> [McConnell] turned his head, he saw me and engaged flaps, with the intent to slow down, to let me pass forward and to riddle me at short range. I realized his maneuver, and sharply broke left, while firing a burst at the Sabre without aiming. The burst struck the base of the right wing, close to the fuselage. A huge hole, about one square meter, appeared in the Sabre's wing. . . . It broke to the right and fell downwards. That was my second enemy destroyed in that combat.

Fedorets was wrong. Though smoking badly and mortally wounded, Captain McConnell's Sabre had just enough fight left in it for him to execute a barrel roll that put him at Fedorets's six (tail) and fire a long burst of machine gun fire that so damaged his MiG that Fedorets was forced to bail out.

Captain McConnell himself had to bail out over the Sea of Japan off the South Korean coast. Air-Sea Rescue had been alerted of Captain McConnell's situation and a rescue helicopter was waiting nearby. It picked him up within two minutes of his splashdown. Captain McConnell later joked that the rescue happened so fast, "I barely got wet."

9 /// VIETNAM: WHERE TOPGUN BEGAN

It's called BVR—"beyond visual range"—and in the early 1960s it had become part of the mantra for a new doctrine of air-to-air combat. Gone was FAGU, the Navy's Fleet Air Gunnery Unit, decommissioned in 1960 and with it the close-in dogfighting tactics it taught. Slated for phaseout as the Navy's top fighter was the single-seat Vought F-8 Crusader, known as the "Last of the Gunfighters" for the brace of four 20mm cannon in its nose. Its replacement, introduced the same year that FAGU was shut down, wasn't another fighter, but an "all-weather, multi-mission" aircraft with a designation that reflected the change in doctrine: interceptor.

With the Cold War then at its height, the Pentagon identified the fleet's main threat in the air to be Soviet bombers. Intercepting them well before they reached the fleet became a priority, which meant designing a warplane and weapon system that could take down the threat of a bomber well before it came into missile range of the fleet. That, in turn, meant that Navy pilots had to shoot down the bombers before their pilots were aware they were under attack; that is, BVR. Because the new doctrine placed the plane beyond the range of 20mm cannon, the new warplane would not be a "fighter" armed with close-in weaponry, but an "interceptor," the first such warplane without a gun system. Instead, it

would be armed with radar-guided Sparrow and heat-seeking Sidewinder air-to-air missiles. The aircraft tapped for this new role as an interceptor was the McDonnell (later McDonnell Douglas) F-4 Phantom II.

Larger, heavier, and more powerful than the Crusader, the Phantom II was also equipped with an advanced radar system that required its own operator, a radar intercept officer (RIO), who sat behind the pilot and managed the battlefield and weapons system while the pilot concentrated on flying the plane.

Because the interceptor's main targets were large, level-flying bombers, training was drastically changed and, thanks to budget restrictions, it included an important modification in the exercise, which we first discussed in Chapter 2.

In this revised training, the F-4 pilot was expected to fly straight and level. When the RIO acquired the BVR, level-flying drone on his radar and chose which missile to shoot, because of budget restrictions, he then *pretended* to fire his Sparrow or Sidewinder. If it was determined that the first shot "missed," the pilot got the F-4 back into position to "fire" a second shot for a "kill."

Then came the Vietnam War.

Suddenly, along with their Marine Corps and Air Force counterparts, F-4 crews found themselves squaring off against a foe for which they had not been trained to fight, operating

aircraft and weapons systems designed for a different style of air-to-air combat and under rules of engagement that contravened the method and purpose of both.

Instead of level-flying bombers, the enemy flew nimble MiG-17 and MiG-21 fighters. And instead of taking aim and shooting at bandits BVR, the new ROE required visual confirmation. Because the MiGs were smaller and thus harder to see, pilots had to get so far inside the lethal cone of their missiles' guidance systems that their own missiles were useless. Then, there was the cockpit design that placed many switches and instruments low in the cockpit, a situation that Captain Ault in his 1969 report called out as requiring the F-4 crew to "fight a heads-up fight with a heads-down system." The result of these and other deficiencies inevitably became tragically apparent in combat.

On April 9, 1965, four Phantoms from VF-96 launched from the USS *Ranger*, which was stationed in the Gulf of Tonkin and near Communist China's Hainan Island. Flying

combat air patrol, the Phantoms were bounced by four MiG-17s originating from one of the island's air bases. In the melee, the F-4s found themselves involved in individual dogfights with the MiGs.

Elements of the after-action report and investigation remain classified to this day, while the information made public leaves what happened murky and controversial. The only thing known for certain is that "Showtime 611," an F-4B flown by pilot Lieutenant (junior grade) Terence M. Murphy and RIO Ensign Ron J. Fegan was shot down and the crew killed in the crash.

The Navy's investigation concluded that Lieutenant Murphy attempted to turn inside a MiG, failed, and was shot down. In 1994, however, Joint Task Force investigator from the Navy was allowed to interview one of the MiG pilots involved in the incident, Captain Li Dayun. He claimed that the MiG pilots did not have permission to use their guns and that Showtime 611 was shot down by friendly fire, a malfunctioning missile.

The theme of malfunctioning missiles only got worse as the conflict escalated.

In May 1968, the Seventh Fleet suffered what came to be called the "*America* Debacle," named after the carrier from which the F-4s flew, a series of F-4/MiG engagements in which Phantoms fired more than thirty Sparrows, successfully shooting down only one MiG but also taking out two Phantoms. By the end of this period, the F-4 kill rate ration had climbed to 2 to 1 (ten MiGs to five Phantoms).

The Crusaders had meanwhile shot down thirteen MiGs (most of them with Sidewinders) at a loss of only three Crusaders to MiGs. Ultimately, the Crusader emerged from the war with the best kill ratio, 19:3.

The Ault Report ultimately revealed that Sparrows had a 63 percent failure rate and, of the remaining 37 percent of successful launches, guidance problems caused 27 percent of them to miss their targets. The Sidewinder was marginally better, with a 56 percent failure rate; of the remaining 44 percent of successful shots, 28 percent missed their target.

The reasons for such dismal results boiled down to two things: aircrew ignorance of missile performance and lack of maintenance. Landing an aircraft on the deck of an

Aircraft handling supervisors from the USS *Constellation* plan the respotting of aircraft to optimize efficient operations on the flight deck prior to mission launch. Such planning can spell the difference between a mission's success or failure.

aircraft carrier has been described as a "controlled crash." The violent impact of aircraft on the deck raised havoc with the missiles' wiring and guidance systems. Maintenance that should have been performed after each sortie was generally not done until after a hundred missions. Meanwhile, in the cockpit, most aircrews had never fired a missile in training and had only the vaguest idea of their weapon's performance or what was required to properly align a target.

The suspension of Navy missions over North Vietnam following the conclusion of Operation Rolling Thunder in October 1968 gave the Navy the breather it needed to fix these and other broken processes. But it took about a year after Topgun graduated its first class before the hoped-for payoff of MiG shootdowns under the new ACM doctrine.

On March 28, 1970, Lieutenant Jerry Beaulier and RIO Lieutenant (junior grade) Steve Barkley of VF-142, the "Ghostriders," were wingmen to Commander Paul Speer on a combat air patrol off the coast of North Vietnam. They were guarding the USS *Constellation* when they got a transmission from a nearby Navy cruiser providing radar coverage and tracking, call sign "Red Crown," notifying them of MiGs 87 miles from their position off the North Vietnamese coast. Flying fast and low, they headed inland to intercept.

Lieutenant Beaulier saw the pair of MiG-21s first, 15,000 feet above and a little to their right (the "one-o'clock-high" position in aviator parlance). Though Commander Speer was senior officer and the section leader, Topgun doctrine emphasized that the person who spotted the bogey or bandit first would get first crack at the enemy, with the other moving back to support.

The pair lit full afterburner and went into a steep climb for the attack. Seeing the Phantoms approach, the MiGs separated, with one climbing in a high arc to the left and the other going into a steep dive. Beaulieu raced after the diving MiG.

Despite violent maneuvers and skillful flying (it was later determined that they were in a dogfight with a squadron leader), Lieutenant Beaulier hung with the MiG and inexorably reduced the distance between the two. He had already armed a Sidewinder, its guidance system emitting a growling noise in his headset as it tracked its prey. Suddenly, the guidance system announced with

a high-pitched whine that it had locked onto the MiG. Lieutenant Beaulier fired. The Sidewinder flew true and exploded beneath the MiG-21. At first he thought he had missed, since the MiG kept flying; as he zoomed over it, it appeared to have suffered nominal damage. But just as he was getting into position for a second shot, fire erupted out of the MiG-21's rear. Not taking chances, Beaulier fired a second Sidewinder at the MiG, destroying it. The other MiG was long gone, having bugged out as soon as contact was made. They returned home to the *Constellation*, where they received a hero's welcome. Back in Miramar, Topgun had learned of the MiG shootdown. Had one of their graduates done it? They were on pins and needles waiting for word one

way or another. When they finally got confirmation that one of "theirs" had done the deed, classes were dismissed for the day and everyone went to the officers' club to celebrate what seen as the beginning of a turnaround for naval aviation—and validation of Topgun.

The celebration turned out to be premature. Topgun graduates failed to score a second shootdown for the rest of 1970, a drought that continued throughout the entire year of 1971. As 1972 began, with the United States on the verge of signing a peace treaty with North Vietnam, it became vital to show that Topgun graduates had scored some kills, and soon, or the program would be shut down.

Hope was rekindled on January 19, 1972, when Lieutenant Randy Cunningham and RIO Lieutenant (junior grade) Bill Driscoll, downed a MiG-2 using two Sidewinders. (Although the maintenance of Sparrows had improved dramatically, Lieutenant Cunningham had enough experience of them failing to distrust them.) Then, on May 8, the pair recorded their second kill, a MiG-17.

It was a "Blue Tree" mission, the codename for "proactive reaction strikes" designed to protect B-52 bombers from MiG attacks. Formed around a RA-5 Vigilante photoreconnaissance aircraft and containing anywhere from thirty-four to forty escort aircraft composed of a mix of A-7 Corsair bombers and F-4 Phantoms, their purpose was to goad the North Vietnamese air force to attack the unarmed Vigilante and Corsairs. When they did, the Phantoms, lurking nearby, would attack.

On that day, the Blue Tree mission included a Vigilante and thirty-five planes. Its objectives were military installations in and around the North Vietnamese settlement of Quan Lang located near the Laotian border. As they approached the target, they armed their bombs and missiles and the force split up; the Phantoms took position in a gigantic circle around the settlement, ready to pounce on the MiGs regardless of their entry point into the area.

Lieutenants Cunningham and Driscoll's Phantom, call sign "Showtime 100," and their wingman were to first fly over a MiG base. They tried to entice the fighters to attack before taking up position north of Quan Lang. Instead of drawing out MiGs, though, they encountered surface-to-air (SAM)

ABOVE: An aerial photograph of the carrier USS *America*. Fighters from this carrier were involved in a disastrous series of missions against MiGs.

RIGHT: A landing signals officer on the flight deck of the USS *Constellation* provides landing instructions to the pilot of an A-4 Skyhawk. He is standing beside a console equipped with a radio communication system, television screen, and radar and other control instruments.

A crewman on the aircraft carrier USS *Hancock* wheels a cart loaded with Sidewinder missiles in preparation for a mission during the Vietnam War.

The MiG-21 (shown here in Romanian livery) was a supersonic fighter widely exported by the Soviet Union from the 1960s to the 1980s. North Vietnam used it during the Vietnam War with great success. Other clients included Warsaw Pact nations (the Eastern European Communist defense counterpart to NATO) such as Romania, as well as India and Indonesia.

missile fire. A total of eighteen deadly missiles crisscrossed the sky as they wove and dodged through the deadly web. Then, almost 4 miles away, Lieutenant Cunningham spotted a pair of MiG-21s. Giving a "Tallyho!" cry indicating he'd spotted bandits and was attacking, he roared off in pursuit. Flying just 200 feet above the ground at 400 miles per hour in a canyon, his plan was to come in fast and low up the MiG's blind spot and nail him with a missile before he knew what hit him.

But the MiG pilot suddenly took evasive action, having somehow been warned of the threat behind and below him. Lieutenant Cunningham hung in with the maneuvering MiG, waiting for the mistake that would give him the opening he needed. The skillful MiG pilot kept frustrating Lieutenant Cunningham. Just as his Sidewinder was about to lock

OPPOSITE: The USS *Constellation* supercarrier (so named for its size) has the distinction of being on station at the beginning of the Vietnam War and at its end.

RIGHT: The flight deck crew of the USS *Constellation* prepares for air operations in the Gulf of Tonkin during the Vietnam War in 1972.

onto the MiG, the pilot would execute a quick maneuver that jockeyed him out of the missile's threat envelope, breaking lock.

Finally, after the MiG had taken a right turn and was about to roll left, Lieutenant Cunningham saw his chance. "Fox Two!" he shouted, announcing that he had fired a Sidewinder at the MiG. The heat-seeker smashed into the MiG's fuselage and blew its tail off. Three down. What were the odds that the crew would bag two more and reach the magic number of five to make ace? Lieutenants Cunningham and Driscoll found out two days later—and then some.

On May 10, again using call sign Showtime 100, the two pilots participated in another airstrike, this time against the Hai Dong railyards. After dropping their bombs, they climbed to assume a combat air patrol position for protecting the other aircraft.

A group of MiG-17s attacked. Lieutenant Cunningham quickly shot down one with a Sidewinder when the MiG overflew his Phantom. Number three. Then, seeing his executive officer (XO) under attack, he repeated three times a call to "break hard." On the third command, the XO did, giving Lieutenant Cunningham a clear shot for his fourth kill.

He was running low on fuel by this point, so he turned away and started heading back to the Constellation. At one point, he saw a MiG in front of him and, despite his fuel state, decided to engage. He wanted that fifth MiG.

The MiG responded aggressively, firing his machine guns and narrowly missing Lieutenant Cunningham's Phantom. He did a hard pull and began a steep climb but, to his surprise, the MiG, whose rate of climb was not as great as the Phantom's, was hot on his tail.

What ensued was a dogfight in which each combatant attempted to use his aircraft's advantages to neutralize the other's. It was a classic "wrestler vs. boxer" fight in which the "wrestler," the MiG, attempted to get in close for the kill while the "boxer," the Phantom, tried to stay at arm's length until an opportunity for attack showed itself.

Back and forth they went, flying high and low, fast and slow, in hard turns and "scissors" maneuvers. Taking shots and missing. Lieutenant Cunningham was down to his last Sidewinder when the MiG suddenly broke off to exit the battle. Lieutenant Cunningham turned swiftly and fired his last Sidewinder. The missile sped true to its target and the MiG disintegrated. Lieutenants Cunningham and Driscoll had their fifth kill and had made ace.

They almost became POWs as well. Hit by a North Vietnamese SAM, Lieutenant Cunningham managed to get his dying Phantom safely over the Gulf of Tonkin, where he and Lieutenant Driscoll ejected and were rescued. For their victories, both received the Navy Cross. Though there was later some dispute, at the time it was widely believed that the pilot of the third MiG they had shot down that day was North Vietnam's greatest ace, the legendary Colonel Nguyen "Toon" Tomb.

LEFT: From left to right: Secretary of the Navy John W. Warner, Lieutenant Randall Cunningham, Lieutenant (junior grade) William Driscoll, and Chief of Naval Operations Admiral Elmo Zumwalt Jr. The pilots are describing the maneuvers they made on the mission where they made ace.

RIGHT: The F-4 Phantom flown by Lieutenant Randy Cunningham and Lieutenant Bill Driscoll when they made ace.

RED FLAG: THE AIR FORCE'S ANSWER TO TOPGUN

Nellis Air Force base in Nevada is home to Red Flag, the Air Force's premier air-to-air and air-to-ground training exercise and counterpart to the Navy's Topgun. Officially known as the US Air Force Weapons School, exercises are held four to six times a year and involve a series of complex, large-force employment missions. These form the capstone of a curriculum that includes the planning and execution of every aspect of air, space, and cyber combat operations, including joint force operations. Exercises have also included aircrews from other nations.

Red Flag was created in 1975 at the recommendation of the Air Force analysis Project Red Baron II, which assessed pilot performance during the Vietnam War. Colonel P. J. White was its first commander, and exercises were first conducted in November 1975.

As with Topgun, the length of its exercises and scope of its curriculum have expanded dramatically to account for ever-changing military threats.

An F-15C Eagle fighter from the Oregon Air National Guard's 123rd Fighter Squadron approaches in-flight refueling during a Red Flag exercise over the Nevada Test and Training Range near Nellis AFB.

OPPOSITE: The French-built Morane-Saulnier monoplane was one of the first true fighter planes. It saw action early in World War I but was soon rendered obsolete by rapid advances in aviation technology due to the war-related innovation.

ABOVE: Roland Garros was already a famous aviator when World War I began, and he became even more famous during the war. The center court of the tennis stadium in Paris, the site of the French Open, is named after him.

For better or worse, wars tend to spur innovation and add to the lexicon. World War I was no exception, the crucible in which use of the airplane as an instrument of death and destruction was tested and perfected. In that conflict, aerial battles came to be known as dogfights because of their resemblance to battles between canines, and aerial maneuvers, such as the Immelmann Turn, were named after the pilots who invented them.

Then there was the conundrum of what to call a pilot who had shot down a significant number of enemy planes. A simple numerical tally of a pilot's score proved unsatisfactory. Just stating that a pilot had shot down five enemy planes lacked panache. A term was needed to add luster in recognition of a pilot's success in shooting planes out of the sky. This is how the word "ace" came into use.

The French press was the first to use the term (*l'As*), bestowing it on Adolphe Pégoud when he shot down his fifth German plane. Initially, though, the British, French, and German air forces set the minimum qualification for "ace" at ten aerial victories (shooting up stationary planes on the ground didn't count). When the United States entered the war in 1917, the minimum was dropped to five, since it was assumed that the latecomer American pilots would be unable to reach the ten-kill minimum. From that point on, five victories became the standard minimum for a pilot to become an ace.

In the early weeks following World War I's outbreak in 1914, pilots on both sides flew unarmed reconnaissance missions over each other's lines. As the prewar fraternity of pilots was a small one, many of those now in uniform knew each other. And, because there was an aura of chivalrous gallantry among these "knights of the air," more often than not they would wave or salute each other as they flew by.

That sense of camaraderie soon vanished. One of the first to take off his gloves, figuratively speaking, was Frenchman Roland Garros. A handsome, glamorous prewar aviator famed for his acrobatic stunts, he won numerous air races and was the first man to pilot a plane across the Mediterranean Sea.

Garros barely avoided starting the war as a POW. Staying in Berlin when war was declared, he managed to slip out of his hotel room before he could be interned and drove to the airfield, where his plane was parked—only to find it surrounded by police. He managed to smooth-talk them into helping gas his plane and roll it out onto the runway. At the time, airplane engines were started by a powerful jerk of the propeller with both hands. This Garros did, quickly climbed into the cockpit, and, taxiing down the runway, flew off into the night. A daring escape, as planes of that era lacked the

necessary instruments to fly in the dark. Garros managed to fly first to Switzerland and then across to France.

Garros was motivated to join the war effort, not out of duty for France or hatred of the Germans, but because he felt the German press had falsely claimed he had been in Germany as a spy. This insult to his honor had to be avenged, and that's what he did.

The next time he went up, flying a Morane-Saulnier monoplane, he was packing a six-shot revolver. Soon he encountered a German Aviatik observation biplane. As he approached, the pilot and observer good-naturedly waved at the Frenchman. He responded by flying wingtip to wingtip with the other plane; he pulled out his revolver, rested it on the edge of the cockpit, took aim, and fired. The German aviators were stunned, then outraged. Garros had emptied his pistol without scoring a single hit, since it was impossible to keep his plane level and steady as he shot at his moving target.

Other attempts at downing enemy aircraft followed. Some involved the threat of slicing off the tail of an opponent's aircraft with the propeller. This was done at considerable risk, over and above the already dangerous aspect of flying, and it was not seriously pursued. For the most part, pilots took flight with pistols, rifles, shotguns—even hand grenades—firing away with abandon, enthusiasm, and little success.

Pusher aircraft were the first to mount a machine gun and shoot down an enemy airplane. The reason was simple: their propellers were set behind the pilot and observer, with forward movement provided by "pushing" the aircraft, thus leaving the front part of the plane clear. Sergeant Joseph Frantz and Corporal Louis Quénault of the French air force, flying a Voisin pusher with a Hotchkiss machine gun mounted beside the observer's cockpit, became the first to shoot down a German plane, an Aviatik B.

LEFT: A French Nieuport fighter. Nieuport was one of France's most important manufacturers in World War I.

RIGHT: The interior of the Nieuport's cockpit. The absence of instruments shows how primitive flying was during World War I.

It happened on October 5, 1914. The two Frenchmen were flying a very crude bombing mission that included lobbing modified artillery shells over the sides of their cockpit onto enemy lines. At one point, they encountered a German scout plane. The Frenchmen flew toward their German adversary and Corporal Quénault, the observer manning the machine gun, fired. After a few rounds, though, the machine gun jammed. Meanwhile, the German observer in the two-man biplane returned fire with a rifle. Corporal Quénault reached down and picked up the rifle he had stowed in the fuselage and began shooting. He scored hits and the Aviatik went into a dive and crashed to the ground, the first aviation kill on record.

Despite their intermittent success, pusher planes using machine guns were limited. Machine guns at this time were heavy, and they often jammed. In addition, the engine and propeller were behind the pilot and observer/gunner: this allowed for a clear view, but shell casings or anything else caught in the slipstream could be flung back and smash into the whirling propellers.

Other plane designs proved equally challenging. A tractor plane, with its engines placed in front and propellers pulling it through the air, did not offer many options for mounting heavy machine guns that could fire forward. The plane's fragile wings couldn't support the weight of the guns, and mounting them beside the fuselage outside the diameter of the whirling propeller was not an option.

At first, machine guns were set above the cockpit on the top wing of the biplane, allowing the machine gun to fire above the propeller. Firing involved pulling a cable mechanism that ran from the trigger to the cockpit. Reloading the ammunition drum was awkward and, frankly, dangerous: the pilot had to loosen his seat belt, get into a half-standing position with the control stick clasped between his knees, pull the machine gun down its rail mount, undo the empty drum, sit down in the cockpit to deposit the old drum in the fuselage, and then grab a new drum. Then he had to reverse the process to load the next rounds.

For Royal Flying Corps pilot Lieutenant Louis Strange, such an operation almost cost him his life. During one sortie in 1914, having exhausted all the ammunition in his machine gun's drum in a failed attempt to shoot down a German plane, Lieutenant Strange began the awkward reloading process. Unfortunately, the drum was jammed onto the machine gun. When he attempted to yank the drum loose, he lost control of his plane, which went into a stall and began spinning.

Still holding onto the drum, Lieutenant Strange was flung out of the cockpit and found himself dangling in the air. Praying that the drum would now *stay* jammed, he somehow managed to get his feet and legs back into the cockpit, pull himself down and regain control of his airplane, and fly safely back to base. After safely landing, his commander reprimanded Lieutenant Strange for "causing unnecessary damage" to the instrument panel of his fighter during his struggle to re-enter the cockpit.

Lieutenant Strange got back into the cockpit and emerged from World War I a decorated fighter pilot. He went on to serve with distinction in the Royal Air Force in World War II.

Meanwhile, Roland Garros was impatient with the state of machine gun technology in aviation. He needed an efficient synchronization firing mechanism that would allow machine guns to shoot forward through a spinning propeller without damaging the blades. No one else had come up with a solution, so he decided to improvise until he found something that worked.

ABOVE LEFT: The Aviatik-B was the first German-designed reconnaissance plane used in the war. Before that, German airplane manufacturers copied French designs. It has the distinction of being the first aircraft to be shot down in war.

ABOVE MIDDLE: A closeup showing a machine gun mounted on the top wing of a World War I fighter. Note the bullet drum and gunsight.

ABOVE RIGHT: Like many airplane designers in the early twentieth century, Anthony Fokker was a skilled pilot.

OPPOSITE: This Nieuport, sporting the livery of the Lafayette Escadrille, has a Lewis gun mounted on its top wing.

OPPOSITE: The Fokker Eindecker ("one wing") was the first fighter plane to use a synchronized machine gun forward-mounted above the engine. An interrupter gear system perfected by Anthony Fokker permitted the machine gun to shoot only when the propeller blades were out of the line of fire.

ABOVE: This formal portrait shows Max Immelmann wearing all his military decorations. The three medals suspended from neck ribbons are the Pour le Mérite (Imperial Germany's highest military decoration for valor), the Cross of the Royal House Order of Hohenzollern (given to officers for bravery in combat), and the Military Order of St. Henry, Commander, 2nd Class. During the war, eighty-one pilots received the Pour le Mérite and 8,300 received the Royal House Order of Hohenzollern. Immelmann was the only one to receive the Military Order of St. Henry, Commander, 2nd Class.

RIGHT: This closeup of the nose of a SPAD S.XIII shows its Vickers machine guns mounted above the engine. When the pilot pulled the trigger, the machine gun fired only when its bullets would clear the propeller.

His idea was to attach protective metal wedges at the base of the wooden propeller shaft and just fire away, playing the percentage that enough bullets would pass between the spinning propellers to hit his intended target. He shared his idea with his old boss, aircraft designer Raymond Saulnier, asking for his help in creating a functional design. And Saulnier did, installing metal wedges around the base of the propeller and doing what he could (which wasn't much) in an attempt to somewhat synchronize the machine gun with the rotating propeller.

The result must have been noisy as hell and pretty darn spectacular, with ricochets flying all over the place in a shower of sparks. On April Fool's Day 1915, Garros took to the air in his monoplane, armed with a single Hotchkiss machine gun mounted over the engine and looking for victims. Soon he spotted a number of German observation craft flying above him. Garros began to climb and position himself at the six (behind the tail) of one of the airplanes. Once he got within range, he pulled the trigger. It took two drums of ammunition, but in the end Garros had scored enough hits to send the enemy plane plummeting to the ground. Together with countrymen Eugène Gilbert and Adolphe Pégoud, Garros began shooting enemy planes out of the sky, racking up victories, and generally causing panic among the German pilots.

But the French air force didn't hold the upper hand for long. Later that April, Garros made the mistake of flying low over German lines. Ground fire so damaged Garros's airplane that he was forced to land behind enemy lines. He was captured before he could set fire to his airplane and its deadly invention. The Germans seized the fighter and handed it over to airplane designer Anthony Fokker.

A Dutchman working for Imperial Germany, Fokker had been studying the problem of machine gun and propeller synchronization for several months before Garros's plane was dropped in his lap. Less than four months later, he had solved the problem: a single synchronized machine gun mounted above the engine of his Fokker Eindecker, immediately transforming the fragile, underpowered monoplane into a deadly killer of the sky.

At least that's what he said. Someone in the group of German commanders shown the contraption must have been from Missouri, or had relatives living there, because Fokker was told, "Show me." He had to don a German pilot's uniform, was provided false identity papers saying he was a German air force pilot, and told to bag a plane. Fokker did take off, and he did encounter some enemy planes, but the fact that he was Dutch and the Netherlands was neutral made him mighty uncomfortable following through with the command. He returned to base and told the real pilots that while he was happy to build deadly fighters, he couldn't bring himself to use one in combat—that was something they would have to do.

The first squadron of Fokker's machine gun–equipped Eindeckers, fifteen in all, went into action in July 1915. Two of the first pilots to get them were Hauptmann (Captain) Oswald Boelcke and Oberlieutenant (First Lieutenant) Max Immelmann. Thus began what the British press called the "Fokker Scourge," in which the deadly German fighters led by Boelcke and Immelman had their way with Allied aircraft for several months, until French and British aircraft designers were able to perfect their own synchronized machine gun systems.

Technological advances changed aerial combat's style but not its substance. Suffice it to say, 1915 was the watershed year in which aerial combat as we know it was born.

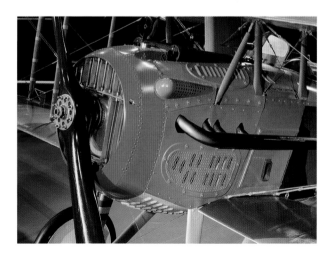

11 GENESIS OF A REVOLUTIONARY DOGFIGHTING TACTIC: THE THACH WEAVE

OPPOSITE: The Grumman F4F Wildcat was the Navy and Marine Corps' top fighter in the beginning of World War II. Though slower and less maneuverable than its main adversary, the Zero, it was more rugged and had more firepower than the Japanese fighter. With proper training, a Wildcat pilot could survive a dogfight with the Zero.

RIGHT: The Messerschmitt Me-163 Komet was the world's first, and only, rocket-powered interceptor, capable of a top speed of 1,000 kilometers per hour. Fortunately for the Allies, it only arrived in combat in 1944, with too few planes and too late to save Nazi Germany in World War II.

The opening years of World War II featured the last hurrah of open-cockpit and fixed-landing-gear warplanes (Japan's Mitsubishi A5M fighter and Aichi D3A "Val" dive bomber) and biplanes (England's Royal Navy Fairey Swordfish torpedo bomber), while the close of the war saw the debut of jet aircraft (Germany's Messerschmitt Me-262 and Me-163b and Heinkel He-162 fighters) and nuclear weapons (the United States's atomic bombs). Throughout, a whole new set of dogfighting tactics appeared, far too many to describe in any depth here. One tactic, though, brought on revolutionary changes to aerial combat. Its creator faced opposition from the Navy and the Army Air Force, but once the tactic was successfully demonstrated in combat, both branches adopted it.

At the start of World War II, senior air commanders in America believed that the Curtiss P-40 Warhawk (Army Air Corps) and Brewster F2A Buffalo and Grumman F4F Wildcat (Navy and Marine Corps) fighters rolling off the assembly lines in the late 1930s offered high enough performance to make the dogfighting tactics of World War I

F4F WILDCAT

The frontline fighter used by the US Navy and Marine Corps for the first eighteen months of the war was the Grumman F4F Wildcat. Though outclassed by its main opponent, the faster and more maneuverable Mitsubishi Zero, the stubby Wildcat was more rugged, capable of sustaining more damage than its more fragile adversary.

Some of the greatest Navy and Marine Corps pilots flew the Wildcat, including Butch O'Hare (for whom Chicago's O'Hare airport is named), Jimmy Thach (creator of the "Thach Weave" defensive maneuver), and Joe Foss (a future governor of South Dakota). All three went on to receive the Medal of Honor.

The Wildcat had some quirks. One of them was that its undercarriage had to be cranked by hand. After takeoff and before landing, ship crews would be greeted with the sight of Wildcats bobbing up and down as the pilot cranked the landing gear handle thirty times to retract or extend the landing gear.

A Grumman F4F Wildcat.

obsolete. Speed trumped maneuverability, in their minds, and each warplane at their disposal could reach speeds well over 300 miles per hour.

Their belief in American air superiority was literally shot down once those fighters clashed with Germany's and Japan's fighters, the Messerschmitt Bf 109 and Mitsubishi Zero, respectively. In one-on-one dogfights, the American fighters didn't stand a chance; Marine Corps fighter pilots bitterly referred to the Buffalo as a "flying coffin."

In their skirmishes with the Japanese in China, the mercenary 1st American Volunteer Group (the "Flying Tigers") demonstrated how it was possible to turn the P-40's few assets—ruggedness, agile low- and mid-altitude performance, power-dive characteristics—to decisive advantage. The group's commander, Brigadier General Claire Chennault, tossed out the manual his Army Air Corps, Navy, and Marine Corps volunteer pilots had trained under, teaching them instead a new set of tactics for their P-40s.

Formations were reconfigured: gone was the three-plane "V"-shaped "vic" formation they had been trained to use, replaced by a two-plane unit. Brigadier General Chennault also trained them to employ a "dive-and-zoom" technique, where pilots only attacked from a superior altitude, with the sun behind them. The wingman provided support for the attacking pilot to make a firing pass at an enemy plane, then continue the high-speed dive to the ground and use his extra speed to fly away. This denied the Japanese pilot the opportunity to use his Zero's superior maneuverability and climb rate to shoot down the Warhawk. This knowledge, bought in blood, was passed on to their counterparts in the States.

Meanwhile, the Navy had already been working on its own change in tactics. As in the Army Air Corps squadrons,

TOP: The Brewster Buffalo proved so outmatched by the Japanese Zero that it was quickly retired. Interestingly enough, Finland's air force had great success with the fighter against the Soviet air force.

BOTTOM: This Brewster Buffalo from VMF-211 crashed onto the flight deck of the escort carrier USS *Long Island* when its landing gear failed. The Marine squadron was the last to operate the Buffalo in frontline capacity.

Navy fighters in the 1930s flew in a "V" formation, with a lead pilot flanked by two wingmen. In October 1939, the same month that World War II began in Europe, Vice Admiral Charles A. Blakely, Commander, Aircraft, Battle Force, a Pacific command based at Pearl Harbor, Hawaii, made a radical change in fighter formation doctrine for the squadrons under his command. Vice Admiral Blakely, an "old man" when he earned his wings at age fifty-four, felt that the three-plane formation had too many disadvantages for the aerial combat he envisioned. He directed that two of the Navy's squadrons, VF-2 and VF-5 (Fighting 2 and Fighting 5, respectively), experiment with two-plane formations. Fighting 2

OPPOSITE: A Chinese soldier stands guard in front of a row of P-40 Warhawks from the American Volunteer Group. It was better known by the name "Flying Tigers" because of the distinctive painting on the fighters' noses, which was done to intimidate Japanese pilots and boost morale among the Chinese.

TOP LEFT: Major General Claire Chennault (shown here after his promotion to that rank) arranged for the War Department to allow him to recruit volunteers from the Army, Navy, and Marine Corps pilots to form the American Volunteer Group, an air force to help China fight Japan.

TOP RIGHT: Vice Admiral Charles A. Blakely was the first senior commander to order changes in dogfight tactics. Ill health forced him to be relieved from active duty on December 9, 1941, two days after the Japanese attack on Pearl Harbor.

RIGHT: The Japanese Zero was used by both the Japanese army and navy in World War II. Like Germany's Messerschmitt Bf-109, it saw service in the war from start to finish. The photo here is that of a captured Zero, thus the US military marking on the fuselage.

further modified the concept by having the wingman fly in a stepped-down pattern, with the idea that it was easier for the wingman to see his leader slightly above and to his left.

This new tactic had immediate and positive results. Nevertheless, when Vice Admiral William Halsey (another "old man" naval aviator, having earned his wings at age fifty-two) succeeded Vice Admiral Blakely in June 1940, he rejected the two-plane formation and ordered the squadrons to return to the "V." In violation of Vice Admiral Halsey's directive, Fighting 2 continued to use the two-plane formation, hoping to convince the admiral to change his mind. Finally, after a series of demonstrations, on July 7, 1941, Halsey reversed his decision and set the two-plane formation for fighters as doctrine. His directive further reorganized Navy squadrons, with each composed of three divisions of six aircraft and each division composed of three two-plane

sections. Rear Admiral A. B. Cook, commander of the Navy's squadrons in the Atlantic Ocean, followed suit a month later.

New formations were built on the two-plane base, with divisions flying into combat in echelon formation before breaking up into individual two-plane sections. Training emphasized the leader's role as attacking plane, while the wingman would provide protection. Unfortunately, in the early stages of the war, some wingmen succumbed to buck fever and broke off to engage the enemy individually, resulting in unnecessary losses.

With the new doctrine in place, the stage was set for one of the great air combat tactical innovations of the war, the Thach Weave.

In the summer of 1941, Lieutenant Commander John S. "Jimmy" Thach, commander of VF-3 (Fighting 3), had established himself as one of the Navy's top pilots and tacticians. In the same month that Vice Admiral Halsey changed formation doctrine, Lieutenant Commander Thach and his command were in San Diego, in the process of exchanging their Brewster Buffalos for new F4F Wildcats. It was there that Lieutenant Commander Thach began receiving intelligence reports from Fleet Air Tactical Unit about the Mitsubishi Zero, along with reports from the Flying Tigers. Lieutenant Commander Thach looked at the performance specs in both reports; although they contained some slight differences, the reports revealed that his enemy would be flying a much better fighter than the new ones he was to receive. The Zero was faster—reaching speeds of up to 380 miles per hour, compared to the Wildcat's 320 miles per hour—and it had an exceptional rate of climb, 3,500 feet/minute compared to the Wildcat's 2,303 feet/minute. Pilots also marveled at the Zero's outstanding maneuverability, seemingly capable of "dancing" through the air.

Unless he could find a way to neutralize and counter the Zero's superior qualities, Lieutenant Commander Thach realized that he'd be sending his pilots on suicide missions. He had a habit of sitting up at night at his kitchen table, developing new tactics with a box of kitchen matches that stood in for possible formations. He was looking for a formation that would be equally strong offensively and defensively, believing that this was the only way to

ABOVE: Admiral William Halsey was the US Navy's most famous admiral in World War II. During the Pacific Ocean campaign against the Japanese, he served as commander of the Third Fleet.

LEFT: From left to right: Lieutenant Edward "Butch" O'Hare and Lieutenant Commander John "Jimmy" Thach. Lieutenant Thach's defensive tactic, the Thach Weave, revolutionized dogfighting.

successfully counter the Zero's superior maneuverability. At first it seemed like an impossible task, running entirely counter to the idea that "the best defense is a good offense."

Almost immediately, though, he saw that his first problem wasn't with the Zero, but with the newly implemented six-plane division. His revelation came when he arranged a four-plane division composed of two two-plane sections. Since flying in close formation made the four planes more vulnerable to attack, he would instead have them fly in a split formation, with the two sections abreast of each other and at distances that represented the Wildcat's turning radius. This formation placed them much further apart than what was called for in existing doctrine. Lieutenant Commander Thach called his new formation the "Beam Defense Position." The key for the tactic's success was locating the aircraft where the pilots were in constant visual contact with each other.

When one two-plane section was attacked, the four-plane division could conduct a "scissors" maneuver in unison, bringing the open section into position to face the enemy aircraft that was attacking its sister section. Suddenly, instead of a head-to-tail engagement, the enemy pilot would confront a head-on attack; he would be forced to decide whether to press on with the fight or break off the engagement.

The idea looked promising, but it needed a real-world test. Lieutenant Commander Thach enlisted one of the best pilots in his squadron, Lieutenant (junior grade) Edward H. "Butch" O'Hare, to lead a "red team" (adversary) of four planes against a four-plane "blue team" (defender), which would be led by Lieutenant Commander himself. To simulate the Zero's superior performance, he had crew chiefs modify the controls on the blue team's Wildcats to reduce their performance.

The two teams then took off and staged a series of mock engagements. Lieutenant O'Hare and his pilots tried every type of attack they knew. In each encounter, they were checked by Lieutenant Commander Thach's Beam Defense Position countermeasure. Despite flying a plane with superior performance, every time Lieutenant O'Hare and his pilots lined up for a shot, they found themselves facing an enemy with an equally good shot at them. When the exercise concluded, they landed and went into the debriefing room. At one point during the debrief, Lieutenant O'Hare told Lieutenant Commander Thach, "Skipper, it really worked. I couldn't make any attack without seeing the nose of one of your airplanes pointed at me."

TOP LEFT: Lieutenant Commander John Thach did more than contribute the Thach Weave maneuver to aerial combat tactics. Later in the war, when the Japanese began using suicide kamikaze air strikes against US Navy fleets, he developed the "big blue blanket" defensive tactic that helped reduce ship losses.

LEFT: An F4F Wildcat test fires its machine guns off the deck of the USS *Enterprise*. Note the open gun bays on the wings and the red circle inside the service livery star on the wings and fuselage. The Navy abandoned the red circle in early 1942 to avoid the chance its planes would be misidentified as Japanese.

When told of Lieutenant Commander Thach's new formation and tactic, Vice Admiral Halsey approved it—but only for Fighting 3. Lieutenant Commander Thach went to work training the rest of the squadron in his Beam Defense Position.

Then history intervened. On the morning of December 7, 1941, the 1st Air Fleet of the Imperial Japanese Navy, under the command of Vice Admiral Chuichi Nagumo, attacked the US Navy harbor at Pearl Harbor and nearby military facilities on the island of Oahu, Hawaii. The United States was now at war. Lieutenant Commander Thach's training of the Beam Defense Position all but stopped, as his experienced pilots were reassigned to other squadrons. He was tasked with conducting a successive series of crash training programs in the basics of combat flying for pilots new to their wings and about to go off and fight in an honest-to-god shooting war.

On May 28, 1942, a group of Navy officers in waders led by Admiral Chester Nimitz, Commander in Chief, Pacific, sloshed through the water draining out of the dry dock and inspected the damaged hull of the carrier USS *Yorktown*, having returned the day before to Pearl Harbor following the Battle of the Coral Sea. Preliminary reports estimated that it would take ninety days to repair the damage suffered in that battle. Looking at the technicians who would lead the work, Admiral Nimitz said, "We must have this ship back in three days." After a long silence, the reply came back, "Yes, sir."

Lieutenant Commander Thach was on Oahu, his Fighting 3 assigned to the *Yorktown*. His command was wholly unlike the squadron he had led in San Diego. The group of pilots before him was very much a mixed bag: a pickup squadron who had never flown together before, some veterans from the *Yorktown* and survivors of the recent battle, some with no recent experience serving on a carrier, and some who had never set foot on a carrier, apart from training takeoffs and landings in Lake Michigan from the paddle-wheel carriers of the Navy's "Corn Belt Fleet." Now he was going to lead them into battle against the Japanese. He didn't yet know where, he only knew that it would be happening soon. The one factor on his side was his XO, Lieutenant Commander Donald Lovelace. An experienced pilot and

capable XO, he had met Lieutenant Commander Thach in Annapolis and they had remained close friends. He was glad to have Lieutenant Commander Lovelace on board.

And then Lieutenant Commander Lovelace was gone. Essential repairs to the *Yorktown* had been completed in

RIGHT: Vice Admiral Chuichi Nagumo commanded the Japanese fleet that attacked Pearl Harbor and Midway. Ironically, he had very little experience with naval aviation, having specialized as a torpedo and destroyer tactician.

BELOW: From left to right: Admiral Raymond Spruance, Vice Admiral Marc Mitscher, Fleet Admiral Chester Nimitz, and Vice Admiral Willis Lee. Nimitz assumed command of the Pacific fleet shortly after Pearl Harbor and helped lead the Navy and Marine Corps to victory against Japan.

A tug approaches the damaged USS *Yorktown* as she arrives at Pearl Harbor following the Battle of the Coral Sea. Instead of returning to the United States, she was hastily repaired so she could assist in the Battle of Midway.

the required three days, and protocol called for the carrier to depart without her squadrons, taking them on only after she was out to sea. As the *Yorktown* received the planes of the Fighting 3 on its first day out, a Wildcat made a bad landing, jumped the barrier, and crashed into the next Wildcat ahead. It was the one piloted by Lovelace, and the crash killed him instantly.

Lieutenant Commander Thach stood before the shaken pilots of his squadron in their briefing room. By now he knew where they were going and what to expect. The fleet that had attacked Pearl Harbor was now about to do the same thing at the Midway Atoll. Calmly, Lieutenant Commander Thach told them of the job they had to do, conveying his strength

and confidence to young men who had so recently been civilians. When he finished speaking, there wasn't a pilot in the room who wouldn't do anything Lieutenant Commander Thach asked.

On June 4, 1942, a contact report from a PBY scout plane was received by Rear Admiral Frank Fletcher. He was overall commander of Task Force 17, made up of the carriers *Enterprise*, *Hornet*, and his flagship, *Yorktown*. Based on the report, Rear Admiral Fletcher ordered the *Enterprise* and *Hornet* to launch a strike against the Japanese fleet, keeping the *Yorktown*'s squadrons in reserve. Two hours later, he gave the order for the *Yorktown* to launch a strike. Twelve torpedo bombers and seventeen dive bombers took

OPPOSITE: A Wildcat being lifted by elevator from the hangar deck to the flight deck in preparation for aerial operations.

BOTTOM LEFT: A two-plane section of F4F Wildcats. Note the prewar color scheme on the fuselage.

BOTTOM RIGHT: Lieutenant Commander Thach became a highly decorated officer in World War II, earning two Navy Crosses, two Navy Distinguished Service Medals, the Silver Star, the Legion of Merit with star and "V" device, and the Bronze Star with "V" device, among other decorations. He went on to serve in the Navy for forty years, retiring in 1967 with the four-star rank of admiral.

off. Protecting them were six fighters led by Lieutenant Commander Thach, the bulk of the fighters remaining for combat air patrol defense to protect the carrier. Lieutenant Commander Thach had talked with the bomber commanders prior to takeoff, and all had agreed that his small force of fighters should provide protection for the slower and more vulnerable torpedo bombers.

The planes took off and headed northwest to find the enemy. At 10:00 a.m. local time, they saw smoke trails on the horizon and immediately began to position themselves for the attack, with the dive bombers climbing to 14,000 feet and the torpedo bombers descending to less than 200, the fighters riding shotgun about 1,500 feet above them.

During his time at Oahu—and especially during their voyage to Midway—Lieutenant Commander Thach had been drilling the pilots on his Beam Defense Position tactic. His theory had worked in exercises, but he never expected

that its first test in battle would be this: an outnumbered and inadequately trained force going up against Japan's most experienced fighters. In an interview conducted years later, he said, "I was utterly convinced then that we weren't coming back."

As the torpedo bombers spread out to make their run, Lieutenant Commander Thach split his command, ordering Machinist Tom Cheek (a naval enlisted pilot) and Ensign Daniel Sheedy to take one side while he led his four-plane division over the other. When they were about 30 miles away from the Japanese fleet, Lieutenant Commander Thach's command was attacked by more than twenty Zeros. Seconds later, he saw one of his Wildcats go down in flames.

He later said, "The air was like a beehive, and I wasn't sure at that moment that anything would work." Suddenly he heard over his headset, "Skipper, there's a Zero on my tail, get him off." It was his wingman, Ensign Ram Dibb.

MITSUBISHI ZERO

Japan's greatest fighter—one of the most outstanding fighters of World War II—was the Mitsubishi Zero, designed by Jiro Horikoshi. Officially designated the Mitsubishi A6M type O, the Zero was used by the Japanese army and navy as its premier fighter throughout the war.

Early on, the Zero easily outperformed its slower, less agile opponents. Because it lacked armor and self-sealing gas tanks, its opponents soon discovered that if they could flame a Zero, it was done for.

One of Japan's greatest aces, credited with sixty-four victories (a number that was later disputed), Saburo Sakai was introduced to the Zero in 1940. He recalled, "The Zero excited me as nothing else had ever done before. Even on the ground it had the cleanest lines I had ever seen in an airplane. . . . The airplane was the most sensitive I had ever flown, and even slight finger pressure brought instant response. We could hardly wait to meet enemy planes in this remarkable new aircraft."

A Mitsubishi Zero.

Lieutenant Commander Thach ordered Ensign Dibb to start the maneuver. As he banked and flew past Lieutenant Commander Thach's F4F, the Zero held on in close pursuit and gave him a perfect, dead-on shot. He pressed the trigger button on his control stick, stitching the Zero with .50 caliber slugs and sending it down in flames.

The sky was filled with enemy planes, and more were on the way. Lieutenant Commander Thach didn't have time to enjoy the success of the maneuver. Issuing a constant stream of orders to his men, he got them to ignore the chaos of battle and focus on executing his maneuver. Their discipline paid off: three more Zeros were shot out of the sky and at least two more were damaged. Equally, if not more importantly, no more Wildcats were lost.

With fuel running low and the attack over, Lieutenant Commander Thach and his four fighters escorted the few torpedo bombers that had survived the attack. Despite grievous losses to the torpedo bomber squadron, things could have been worse—his command might have been annihilated. But, thanks to his Beam Defense Position tactic, his Wildcats had outfought the Zero. So the tactic worked—or did it? In late October 1942, Lieutenant Commander Thach got an unequivocal answer, one that put him in the history books.

Shortly before he arranged his squadron on the *Yorktown*, he had discussed the tactic with his friend, Lieutenant Commander James Flatley, who had led a *Yorktown* fighter squadron in the Battle of the Coral Sea. He was about to return to the States to command a new squadron, VF-10, soon to earn fame in the war as the "Grim Reapers." Lieutenant Commander Flatley liked Lieutenant Commander Thach's idea, initially preferring a six-plane formation, but later opting for the four-plane variation.

VF-10 was assigned to the *Enterprise* and soon found itself in the thick of the campaign to wrest the Southwest Pacific island of Guadalcanal from the Pacific. A brutal campaign that lasted for months, one of the many naval engagements was the costly Battle of the Santa Cruz Islands off the coast of Guadalcanal on October 24, 1942. At the end of the day on October 26, Lieutenant Commander Flatley was leading his exhausted squadron home to the

Enterprise after an attack on the Japanese fleet. Everyone was low on fuel, and Lieutenant Commander Flatley himself was out of ammunition. Without warning, they were attacked by a strong force of Zeros. The commander initiated Lieutenant Commander Thach's weaving tactic. Despite repeated attempts by the Japanese fighters (and the fact that he had no way to fight back), Lieutenant Commander Flatley survived all the enemy's efforts to shoot him down, and he and his squadron escaped. In his after-action report, he described his harrowing brush with death and how he survived by using the Beam Defense Position. In recognition of the man who taught him the maneuver he wrote, "the four-plane division is the only thing that will work, and I am calling it the Thach Weave." Lieutenant Commander Thach's tactic was soon adopted throughout the Navy and picked up by the Army Air Force as well. The Thach Weave proved adaptable, resulting in a number of spinoffs.

12 "AERIAL DOGFIGHTING IS DEAD"

OPPOSITE: The Vought F-8 Crusader, nicknamed "The Last of the Gunfighters," beat out McDonnell for the Navy day fighter contract. McDonnell would get its revenge with the Phantom II.

RIGHT: Two F-4 Phantoms escort a Soviet Tupolev Tu-16 bomber, codenamed "Badger." Together with the Tupolev Tu-95, codenamed "Bear," these were the bombers the Phantom was designed to intercept and shoot down.

The 1950s saw breathtaking advances in warplane technology. Within a decade, aircraft design went from subsonic turboprop to supersonic jet, reaching for the magic goal of Mach 3.

The Cold War had encouraged such urgency. An ideological conflict between Western democracies (led by the United States) and Communism (led by the Soviet Union), it played out largely on the battlefields of surrogates like Korea and Vietnam. These theaters of war served as platforms where conventional forces dueled for supremacy, with the United States and the Soviet Union holding their nuclear weapons at the ready as the ultimate counterstroke.

To keep the Cold War from going hot, the Eisenhower administration of the 1950s relied on the deterrence doctrine of massive retaliation, "mutual assured destruction" (MAD), where any use of nuclear weapons by the Soviet Union would be met with an all-out nuclear response by the United States. In this climate, the Air Force and (to a lesser extent) the Navy sought fighter and bomber designs they could operate in a strategic nuclear environment, supporting offensive nuclear operations or defending against nuclear attack.

This caused a complete shift in the philosophy of aircraft design. Maneuverability and sustained sortie rates would be sacrificed to achieve greater speed, ceiling, payload, range, and penetration. Bombers were integral to the delivery of nuclear payloads, which meant that manufacturers of these aircraft received more attention—and support, in the form of money for research and development. The result was the B-52 Stratofortress. Introduced in 1955, it remains operational to this day as the longest serving military aircraft in aviation history.

The Air Force financed all manner of designs in search of the "ultimate fighter." The more successful entries were

North American's F-100 Super Sabre, a supersonic next-generation F-86 Sabre, Vought's twin-tailed F7U-3 Cutlass, Convair's delta-winged F-106A Delta Dart, Lockheed's stubby straight-winged F-104 Starfighter, and Republic's F-105 Thunderchief.

Just as in the early months of World War II, the onset of the Korean War demonstrated that the United States's top fighters were inferior to those of the enemy. But the Navy was determined not to be caught flatfooted again. Even so, the branch was slow to develop its own ultimate fighter. Aviation was only part of its defense posture, unlike the Air Force. This meant that precious R&D dollars had to be portioned out between new designs for aircraft along with money for nuclear submarines, aircraft carriers, and other ships. In addition, the R&D costs ballooned in the face of technological challenges associated with designing a

high-performance, supersonic aircraft capable of sustained takeoffs and landings from a carrier deck.

The US Navy offered two contracts in 1953, one for its first all-weather supersonic fighter, the other for a supersonic day fighter. Grumman, the Navy's primary aircraft contractor since the 1930s, received the all-weather fighter contract. Douglas Aircraft might have been the natural choice to build the day fighter, since it had built more than one thousand aircraft for the Navy, including the straight-wing FH-1 Phantom jet fighter; however, it lost out to Vought (of World War II F-4U Corsair fame) for that contract. As it turned out, Grumman's design failed, and Vought's became the F-8 Crusader, leaving a gap in the Navy's aviation inventory.

McDonnell Aviation was also interested in doing work for the Navy. Chairman James "Mr. Mac" McDonnell headed what had been a second-tier naval aviation contractor, but

JAMES SMITH MCDONNELL JR.

He was one of the giants of aviation: "Mr. Mac," as he was known with respect, admiration, and awe. James S. McDonnell Jr. had earned his pilot's wings from the Army Air Service in the 1920. An aeronautical engineer by training, in 1939 he founded McDonnell Aviation in St. Louis.

Timing was everything. When World War II broke out, his company was ready to supply the Department of War's needs. Within three years, his company had grown so large that it was the chief industry in St. Louis, outpacing the Anheuser-Busch brewery.

In an industry filled with powerful egos, McDonnell stood out. With his knowledge and executive control of McDonnell Aviation, he literally *was* the company. Nobody forgot that he called the shots, literally, as the following anecdote illustrates.

The company was planning a small employee party. One of the planners asked how much liquor should be purchased. Mr. Mac immediately pulled out his slide rule, figured exactly two and one-quarter drinks per person, and calculated *precisely* how many bottles of liquor should be ordered.

he was determined to remain in the game and establish his company as a major player. He ordered his executives, designers, and engineers into an all-out effort to uncover the Navy's expectations for the next generation of fighter. This included gathering intel from Bureau of Aeronautics officers, the CNO, and anyone else involved in naval aviation, down to pilots and their crews. In 1954, McDonnell Aviation submitted a design for the AH-1, a single-seat, cannon-armed attack aircraft. The Navy found the design promising and gave McDonnell seed money for a prototype. The following year, the Navy turned that design inside-out and upside-down.

The request was for McDonnell to scrap the AH-1 design and replace it with a two-seat, missile-armed, long-range, high-altitude interceptor. This new design would be used primarily for fleet defense against Soviet bomber attack.

The cockpit of an F-4 Phantom II shows how complex flying the interceptor could be, a far cry from the few instruments found in a World War I fighter.

It should be able to cruise out to a radius of 250 nautical miles, stay on combat patrol, attack an intruder from long range (BVR) when necessary, and return to the carrier in three hours. The only thing retained from the original design was its swept-wing profile. The aircraft's designation was changed from AH-1 to F4H-1.

A second crew member would sit behind the pilot to handle all the additions the Navy wanted packed into the interceptor: state-of-the-art radar, missile fire control, advanced navigation systems, an analog air-data computer, a network of onboard senses from nose to tail, and more. In all, there were 30,000 electronic parts, many of them new, connected by 14 miles of wiring. It was far too much for one pilot to handle *and* fly and fight. That backseater, as he came to be called, was designated a "weapon system operator" (WSO) or "radar intercept officer" (RIO). The pilot would fly and shoot, while the WSO/RIO would be responsible for everything else. Vought, determined to keep McDonnell off what it regarded as its turf, began work on a new design.

A competition fly-off was held in 1958 between McDonnell's interceptor entry, now designated the F-4 Phantom II, and Vought's, the F8U-3 Crusader III. The goal was to see which would be named the Navy's next primary interceptor. The F-4 Phantom II won. Later added to the Air Force's inventory, the plane went on to become the military jet aircraft that defined the 1960s. H. D. Barkey, vice president of the Aircraft Engineering Division at McDonnell, noted the irony of the Phantom's success when he said, "The Phantom had its beginning not by winning an aircraft competition, but rather by losing one."

On the day that the Phantom II was selected, George Spangenberg, an official in the Navy Bureau of Aeronautics, declared, "The single-seat fighter era is dead." He might have added something else to his proclamation: the Crusader III was built to carry four 20mm cannon; the Phantom II was not. Additionally, as a cost-saving measure, its air crews weren't allowed to familiarize themselves with their new armament by firing missiles in training.

13 // THE QUESTION OF STEALTH

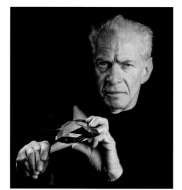

In June 1977, something at Lockheed Martin's Skunk Works in Burbank, California, was making top Air Force generals giddy. The operation, the same that had designed the U-2 and SR-71 Blackbird spy planes, was now readying a new prototype aircraft under the codename Have Blue. The word had gotten out about this new plane, to the degree that President Jimmy Carter's national security council chief, Dr. Zbigniew Brzezinski, flew to Burbank to see it for himself. Had the Skunk Works achieved the Holy Grail of military aviation? Had they designed a stealth aircraft, one invisible to radar?

The Have Blue program was deemed so important that it received the classification "Top Secret/Special Access Required," putting it in the same rarefied category as World War II's Manhattan Project, the group that had built the atomic bomb.

Brzezinski was met by the Skunk Works's director, Ben Rich, who had succeeded legendary aircraft designer and Skunk Works founder Kelly Johnson two years earlier. Rich escorted the National Security Council chief to a classified hangar and unveiled something that looked like a sculpture created by Georges Braque or Pablo Picasso during their Cubist periods: Have Blue. With Rich in tow, Brzezinski did a walkaround of the aircraft, asking question after question about the radical new design.

Hours later, as he was preparing to return to Washington, Brzezinski turned to Rich and asked the $350 million question: "If I were to accurately describe the significance of this stealth breakthrough to the president, what should I tell him?" Rich replied, "Two things. It changes the way that air wars will be fought from now on. And it cancels out all the tremendous investment the Russians have made in their defensive ground-to-air system. We can overfly them at any time, at will."

Before Have Blue, military and civilian aircraft design was based on aerospace engineering, which focuses on how an aircraft performs in relation to atmospheric conditions around it. Have Blue was the first aircraft designed according to radar engineering, predicated on how it performed against detection by electromagnetic radiation (radar).

Conventional military aircraft have large radar signatures and rely on speed, maneuverability, or defensive measures like chaff (strips of aluminum foil) or flares to avoid or confuse radar-guided missiles. In contrast, a stealth aircraft's defense against missile attack is its radar invisibility.

We can compare the Have Blue aircraft with standard jet planes being produced at the time. For example, an F-14 Tomcat was about 62 feet long, 16 feet high, had an open wingspan of 64 feet (38 feet swept), and weighed about 61,000 pounds with fuel. Its radar signature was, figuratively speaking, big as a barn. The Have Blue proof-of-concept prototype was just over 47 feet long, just under 8 feet high, had a wingspan of about 22 feet, and had a gross weight of 12,500 pounds; it was roughly a quarter-scale of the eventual production model, the F-117-A Nighthawk. According to Denys Overholser, a member of the Have Blue design team, its faceted surface and radar-dampening materials meant that Have Blue's radar signature was "as big as an eagle's eye."

Introduced in 1983, the F-117-A Nighthawk first saw combat in 1989 in Operation Just Cause, the invasion of Panama that deposed strongman General Manuel Noriega; two Nighthawks conducted bombing missions during that conflict. But the aircraft's real test came three years later against Iraq and its dictator, Saddam Hussein, during Operation Desert Shield/Desert Storm.

At the time, Iraq possessed the most sophisticated integrated air defense system (IADS) outside the United States and the Soviet Union. Consisting of almost twenty different types of radar systems, the network was run by a French-built command, control, communication (C3) system called KARI (the French word for "Iraq" spelled backwards). When France became a member of the Desert Shield/Desert Storm military coalition, the contractor who built it provided invaluable intelligence about its locations and capability.

Though its deployment in the Panama operation had been a success, a definitive test of the Nighthawk would have to wait for Desert Storm, the 1991 invasion of Iraq. A Nighthawk squadron would lead the charge at the kickoff of this operation—but was the F-117A Nighthawk stealthy enough to slip through Iraq's sophisticated radar system and complete its missions? Desert Shield, the leadup to Desert Storm, included F-117A flights just inside the Iraqi-Saudi border; these had apparently not been detected by KARI, but nobody knew for certain. Now, as the shooting war commenced, everyone would soon find out.

On January 17, 1991, at 12:22 a.m. local time, ten F-117As from the 415th Tactical Fighter Squadron of the 37th Tactical Fighter Wing (Provisional) took off from Khamis

Mushait in southern Saudi Arabia and headed north to attack sixteen high-value targets, mostly in and around Baghdad, which had the heaviest concentration of antiaircraft defenses. Upon their return, the planes had severely damaged or destroyed all assigned targets without a loss—and without being detected.

The Gulf War ended on February 28, 1991. In a little over a month of combat, the F-117A had flown 1,300 sorties and scored direct hits on 1,600 high-value targets without suffering a single loss.

By the time it was retired from service on April 22, 2008, only one F-117A had been lost in combat, an astonishing success rate. (It was replaced by two stealth aircraft: the F-22 Raptor and the F-35 Lightning II Joint Strike Fighter.) We may wonder how an aircraft, which was nearly 100 percent invisible to radar, could be shot down. Well, because it *wasn't* 100 percent invisible to radar, just 99.99 percent, when its bomb bay doors were closed; when the doors were open, the Nighthawk was just as visible on radar as any conventional airplane.

That brief window of vulnerability was dramatically exposed on the night of March 27, 1999. In Operation Allied Force, NATO employed F-117As in its air bombing campaign against the Federal Republic of Yugoslavia (containing Serbia

The design of Lockheed Skunk Works' Have Blue proof-of-concept aircraft was unprecedented. Specifically designed to thwart detection by radar, it was the first aircraft to incorporate stealth technology.

LOCKHEED F-117A NIGHTHAWK

The F-117A Nighthawk is the world's first operational aircraft completely designed around stealth technology. It has a crew of one, a maximum speed of 700 miles per hour, and contains two internal weapons bays capable of carrying a variety of laser-guided bombs and missiles. It became operational in 1983 and was retired from the Air Force in 2008.

One of the most vivid images of an F-117A attack during Operation Desert Storm showed a Nighthawk deliver a precision-guided bomb down the airshaft of the Iraqi Defense Ministry building. Air Force Colonel Barry Horne, an F-117A pilot during the campaign, had confirmation of the Nighthawk's stealth capability from an unexpected source. He recalled, "The Saudis provided us with a first-class fighter base with reinforced hangars, and at night the bats would come out and feed off insects. In the mornings, we'd find bat corpses littered around our airplanes inside the open hangars. They were crashing blindly into our low-radar-cross-section tails."

The F-117A Nighthawk was the first stealth aircraft. It became operational in 1983 and served in the US Air Force for twenty-five years before being retired in 2008. Though called a "stealth fighter," it was used as a ground attack warplane. During the design process, because its shape was so radically different than that of any previous aircraft, it was nicknamed the "Hopeless Diamond."

OPPOSITE: The F-117A Nighthawk was the first stealth aircraft. It became operational in 1983 and served in the US Air Force for twenty-five years before being retired in 2008. Though called a "stealth fighter," it was used as a ground attack warplane. During the design process, because its shape was so radically different than that of any previous aircraft, it was nicknamed the "Hopeless Diamond."

RIGHT: This reconnaissance photo taken the day after shows the result of a night strike by F-117A Nighthawks against reinforced concrete aircraft bunkers at the Ahmad Al Jaber Airfield in Iraq during Operation Desert Storm.

BELOW: The cockpit of a Nighthawk. The stealth aircraft's design was so complex, a pilot couldn't even taxi it without computer assistance.

and Montenegro and claiming to be the successor state to Yugoslavia, which had disbanded in 1992). Although NATO leaders regarded it as obsolete, the Yugoslav air defense system had secretly modified its Soviet-built air defense radar, allowing for detection of the F-117A under certain conditions. Yugoslav military intelligence had learned the flight pattern used by F-117As; also, it must be remembered that, though the Nighthawk was invisible to radar, it could still be seen by the naked eye. The Yugoslav military was thus prepared to meet the bombers, having placed their mobile antiaircraft artillery batteries in strategic locations to better exploit what they knew about the NATO planes' vulnerability.

A little after 8:15 p.m. local time, Lieutenant Colonel Dale Zelko, call sign Vega-31, saw two SAMs rocket out of the cloud cover below him and head for his Nighthawk. The first one narrowly missed him, but the second didn't. Lieutenant Colonel Zelko successfully bailed out of the stricken aircraft and was rescued before he could be captured.

While the value of stealth technology is unquestioned, Zelko's shootdown proved that it would be a mistake to believe it was infallible.

While the Air Force was dominating the skies with stealth technology, where was the Navy? Actually, the Navy's foray into stealth had preceded the Air Force's by decades, using it in its submarines. The Navy's *Ohio*-, *Los Angeles*-, and *Seawolf*-class submarines are the stealth standard by which all others are measured. The branch has also invested heavily in drone technology for its ships and boats. When it came to applying stealth to its warplanes, though, the Navy would have to wait to retire one of its active aircraft—the F-14 Tomcat, F-16 Fighting Falcon, or F/A-18 Hornet and Super Hornet fighters—before buying a next-generation aircraft. That came at last in 2016 with its purchase of the F-35A Lightning II.

In the meantime, the Navy invested in its Unmanned Carrier Launched Surveillance and Strike (UCLASS) program as a way of combining stealth technology with its drones.

14 // THE NAVY AND AERIAL DRONES

For many years, top military leaders have been cursed with the axiom that they were always prepared to fight the last war, a statement that is unfortunately proven by history. The same cannot be said of today's admirals and generals who have embraced a cornucopia of new technologies. Arguably, the face of the new war-making landscape is the unmanned aerial vehicle (UAV—unarmed, reconnaissance) and the unmanned combat aerial vehicle (UCAV—armed, combat capable), more popularly known as drones. Their impact cannot be overstated. Indeed, the Pentagon has announced that the F-35A Lightning II Joint Strike Fighter will be its last manned fighter. After that, all aerial combat will be conducted by pilots sitting in a room on the ground, staring at a flat screen while operating a variation of a computer game controller. While this doesn't mean Topgun will go out of business soon, at some time in the future the program may find itself flying off into the sunset.

Though the Navy was slow to add drones to its arsenal, tradition hasn't been the source of this resistance. Instead, it comes down to a practical matter: the platform on which drones would take off and land. It's one of the most important things that separates US Navy and Marine pilots from their Air Force counterparts. Air Force pilots take off and land from large airfields built on unmoving ground, whereas Navy and Marine pilots do so from a bobbing aircraft carrier flight deck that's relatively the size of a postage stamp. It takes enormous technological and training resources to take off and land from such a vessel. To pilot a drone in such maneuvers is equally challenging, and it took years before drone technology had reached the necessary level.

On May 10, 2013, naval aviation history was made when the stealth UAV X-47B made by Northrop Grumman took off from the deck of the USS *George H. W. Bush*. It was a feat as important as Eugene Ely's flight off the makeshift deck of the cruiser USS *Birmingham* on January 18, 1911. Two months later, on July 10 (again on the USS *George H. W. Bush*), an X-47B made a successful landing on a carrier. Navy Secretary Ray Mabus was there to watch the test; he reported afterward: "It is not often that you get a chance to see the future, but that's what we got to do today. This is an amazing day for aviation in general and for naval aviation in particular."

Because of their explosive proliferation in recent years, it seems as if drones are a new thing. In fact, drones have been around for more than 150 years. The first drone, an unmanned hot-air balloon, was used in the 1850s. Though they made periodic appearances over battlefields, their first meaningful impact didn't occur until World War II. These

ABOVE: General Ronald Fogleman flew 315 combat missions during the Vietnam War. It was during his tenure as Air Force chief of staff that the Air Force extensively increased its use of drones.

LEFT: The F-35 Lightning II is a Joint Strike Fighter, which means the stealth fighter is designed for use by the Air Force, Navy, and Marine Corps. The Navy and Marine Corps variants are built sturdier to tolerate hard landings on aircraft carriers. The Pentagon has said it will be their last manned fighter.

OPPOSITE: The RQ-1 Predator drone in its UCAV variant. Armed with two Hellfire missiles, it is the most famous of the military drones.

efforts included the Army Air Force's tragic Operation Aphrodite, which used modified B-17 drones packed with explosives in an attempt to destroy German V-2 rocket bases. They revealed, however, that the technology was still too primitive for practical implementation. The Vietnam War saw the first widespread use of drones, both on the battlefield and in training. As the technology matured, their military use expanded; even so, drone use had yet to realize its full potential.

That potential was finally achieved on July 29, 1995, when Air Force Chief of Staff General Ronald R. Fogleman activated the 11th Reconnaissance Squadron. Its aircraft? The RQ-1 Predator UAV.

Though the military employs a wide variety of drones—some as small as a dragonfly, others weighing thousands of pounds—the Predator is arguably the "face" of modern military drones. Designed and developed by Israeli émigré Abraham Karem in the 1980s, it was initially unarmed. Its first

GENERAL ATOMICS
PREDATOR

The Predator and its UAV and UCAV variants are the best known of all military drones. The term "Predator" doesn't officially refer to the aircraft itself; instead, it indicates a weapon systems package that includes four aircraft (with assorted sensor packages); a ground control station; a secure satellite communications link; an operations crew composed of a pilot and one or two sensor operators; and a maintenance and support crew containing as many as fifty-two mechanics and technicians.

As with all drones, Predators don't carry a pilot and life support systems, which means they're substantially smaller, lighter, and cheaper than manned aircraft. Of course, this also means that risk of death, injury, or capture of the crew is minimal, because the Predator is controlled by the pilot and control station operators on the ground, and in some cases half a world away. As more new Predators, UAVs, and UCAVs come into service, they stand to do something once thought impossible: sweep the skies clear of piloted warplanes.

A crew chief prepares an MQ-1B Predator for a training mission. Note the missile mounted under its left wing.

An F/A-18E Super Hornet conducts in-flight refueling operations with an EA-18G Growler. With up to 30 percent of its missions devoted to refueling, the Navy is anxious to find a more efficient alternative.

military application took place in 1999, when it was used to conduct reconnaissance in Operation Allied Force, the NATO campaign to protect Kosovo from Serbian conquest. Success there led to the development of a Predator armed with a Hellfire missile, thus changing its designation from UAV to UCAV ("C" for "combat").

While the drone remained classified for several years, that secrecy was brought to a dramatic end on November 3, 2002, when Predator UCAVs were used to attack and kill Qaed Salim Sinan Al-Harethi, a senior Al Qaeda leader and mastermind of the bombing of the USS *Cole* in Yemen. The Predator was soon joined by the larger MQ-9 Reaper UCAV and the reconnaissance drone RQ-4 Global Hawk, among others.

Studying how drones could best fit its needs, the Navy soon identified an important weakness in its inventory: aircraft for in-flight refueling. Fighter jets consume enormous amounts of fuel, and Navy jets, because they use their afterburners for carrier takeoffs, consume even more. This limited their range and effectiveness.

The Navy's last purpose-built tanker was the Grumman KA-6D Intruder, retired from service in 1997. Since then, the Navy has used F/A 18 Super Hornets equipped with external fuel tanks for refueling or, on rare occasions, assistance from the Air Force's tanker fleet. It is at best an imperfect solution.

Tasking fighters for tanker missions takes them away from their attack role, reducing a squadron's overall combat strength (along with shortening the operational life of those fighters tasked for the dual role).

Air Force tanker assistance comes with a host of problems, beginning with the fact that, naturally, the Air Force prioritizes its tankers to refuel Air Force planes. The problems go deeper, though: the services use two different types of jet fuel—the Navy uses JP-5, while the Air Force uses JP-8—*and* they have two different delivery systems; the Navy's "hose-and-drogue" delivery is incompatible with the Air Force's "flying boom." This means that, whenever Air Force tankers get tasked to support Navy aircraft, the tankers have to flush their fuel cells to clean them and change their delivery systems. The intensity of air combat operations over Iraq and Afghanistan has placed enormous stress on Navy refueling operations. Clearly a solution must be found.

After years of fits and starts, in 2016 the Navy requested contractors to submit proposals for what would become the MQ-25A Stingray stealth tanker. The delay leading up to that breakthrough was largely due to back-and-forth discussion about whether the aircraft would be UCLASS (unmanned carrier-launched airborne surveillance and strike—"combat") or CBARS (carrier-based aerial refueling system—"support"). The decision was finally made on CBARS, and request for proposals went out.

Regarding basic requirements, the Navy stated,

> For mission tanking, the threshold requirement is offloading 14,000 lbs. of fuel to aviation assets at 500 nm from the ship, thereby greatly extending the range of the carrier air wing, including the Lockheed Martin F-35C and Boeing F/A-18 Super Hornet. The UAV must also be able to integrate with the *Nimitz*-class carriers, being able to safely launch and recover and not take up more space than is allocated for storage and repairs.

Boeing, Lockheed Martin, and General Atomics submitted proposals. But the X-47B UAV that took off and landed on the *George H. W. Bush* in 2013 was built by Northrup Grumman, who subsequently dropped out of the competition. Both the *George H. W. Bush* and the *Dwight D. Eisenhower* will be upgraded to make them capable of operating the stealth tanker UAV. Because as much as 30 percent of all Super Hornet sorties are tanker missions, CNO Admiral John Richardson has placed the entire program on a fast track. In August 2018 the Navy announced that winner for the contract was Boeing and that the first four drones will be operational in 2024.

The military uses the term "force multiplier" to describe the increase in effectiveness and capability of a group or weapon system. Another concept, "distributed lethality," may be put into practice by equipping every warship capable of launching and receiving helicopters with a squadron of drones, making them mini-aircraft carriers. Thus, instead of

thirty-one carriers (eleven *Nimitz*-class supercarriers, like the one featured in *Top Gun*, and twenty smaller amphibious assault ships), and when combined with warships containing helicopter decks, the Navy could have as many as 282 "carriers" at a fraction of the cost.

Truly a mind-boggling concept.

BELOW: An MV-22 Osprey prepares to land on the deck of the carrier USS *George H. W. Bush*. Originally designed as a Vertical Takeoff and Landing aircraft, in-flight refueling tests are scheduled to begin in 2019 with the goal of being operational in 2020.

RIGHT: An X-47B being prepared for takeoff from the flight deck of the USS *Theodore Roosevelt* on November 11, 2013. The Navy plans to use it in place of Hornets and Super Hornets for refueling operations.

15 FIGHTERTOWN, USA, HEADS TO NEVADA

ABOVE: The insignia of Miramar in 1948, when it was designated a Naval Auxiliary Station.

OPPOSITE: A pair of F-35 Lighting IIIs and a pair of F/A-18 Super Hornets fly in formation somewhere in the airspace above Naval Air Station Fallon.

On May 29, 1996, one era of the Navy Fighter Weapons School history closed and another one opened. Four F-14 Tomcats and twelve F/A-18 Super Hornets took off from Mitscher Field in Naval Air Station Miramar and headed east to their new home, Naval Air Station Fallon, near Reno, Nevada. When they left, the Navy base commander gave the "keys" to the base to its new owner. Naval Air Station Miramar, once known as Fightertown, USA, was no more, victim to a decision made by the Base Realignment and Closure (BRAC) Commission that periodically reviews military base status. From that point on, it would be known as Marine Corps Air Station Miramar.

Constructed in the high desert of Nevada in 1942, the new Fightertown, USA, had originally served as a backup Army Air Corps air base in World War II. It was part of the Western Defense Program to counter a possible Japanese invasion of the West Coast. In 1943, the Navy took ownership and used it to train pilots for combat. It was commissioned Auxiliary Air Station Fallon on June 10, 1944. It reached its height of training operations in summer 1945, averaging 21,000 takeoffs and landings and logging more than 12,000 hours of flight time. Following Japan's surrender in September 1945,

Naval Auxiliary Air Station Fallon's status rapidly declined, going from "reduced operation status" following the end of the war to "maintenance status" on February 1, 1946, to "caretaker status" that June, when its NAAS designation was removed. Its facilities were then used by the Bureau of Indian Services for the next five years.

Fallon was reactivated with the onset of the Korean War, and from that point on its role in the Navy grew. In recognition of its expanding importance, on January 1, 1972, its status was upgraded to Naval Air Station Fallon.

With a much bigger playground (240,000 acres, compared to 23,116 at Miramar), Topgun could now conduct full carrier air wing exercises—something it had never been able to do; in fact, something no other similar military base in the world to this day can do.

With a change of location came a change in the station's table of organization—and a new name. Now integrated with the Naval Strike and Air Warfare Center (now the Naval Aviation Warfighting Development Center, or NAWDC) and commanded by an admiral, Topgun's new official name was United States Navy Strike Fighter Tactics Instructor program.

More than 600 pilots and their family members made the move from Miramar—or from the major urban center of San Diego and its environs—to Fallon, a small town of about

8,000 people located in the Nevada desert. For the pilots, it was familiar territory, as Fallon's status as a hub for naval aviation meant that they had all been stationed there at one point in their career.

Topgun's incorporation into the new command meant an expansion of its air-to-ground strike curriculum. It had originated as a four-week course narrowly focused on training F-4 Phantom crews to combat Soviet MiGs, combined with a short air-to-ground lesson plan. In its new version, the course included extra time to address the changes in air combat, something that continues to this day.

In its present manifestation, Topgun conducts four "Power Projection" classes a year. Each strike fighter tactics instructor (SFTI) course lasts about nine weeks and covers all aspects of strike fighter aircraft operations, including tactics, hardware, techniques, and current-world air-to-air and air-to-ground missions. The course includes eighty hours of lectures and twenty-five sorties against Topgun instructors.

Included in each class are four to six Air Intercept Controllers (AIC). As with the fighter pilots and WSOs, the

The F-5 Tiger II's similarities in performance to Russian fighters makes it useful for Topgun instructors in their aggressor role. Note the red star on its tail, indicating that it is an aggressor.

Lieutenant Colonel Dave Berke, USMC (Ret.), a Topgun student and, later, instructor.

TOPGUN'S FIRST FEMALE FIGHTER PILOT

TOPGUN'S FIRST FEMALE FIGHTER PILOT

In 1993, Secretary of Defense Les Aspin lifted the orders that prohibited women from serving as fighter pilots. That year, twelve female seniors at the US Naval Academy qualified for such billets. With that hurdle overcome, it was only a matter of time before a woman was enrolled at Topgun. That happened in 2004, when Commander Becky Calder became the first woman fighter pilot to be accepted into the Topgun program.

A 1998 graduate of the US Naval Academy, Commander Calder earned her wings in 2000 and became an F/A-18 Super Hornet fighter pilot. Two years later, she found herself flying air support combat missions over Afghanistan in Operation Enduring Freedom.

After graduating from Topgun, she became an instructor at the Strike Fighter Weapons School Atlantic. An active-duty pilot for fourteen years, she has the distinction of being one of the few pilots to have flown every variant of the F/A-18. She logged 2,500 hours of flying time and made 421 arrested landings, 185 of them at night.

Lieutenant Colonel Dave Berke, USMC, (Ret.), was an F/A-18 pilot who was accepted into Topgun in 2001 and who later became an instructor in the program. He noted,

> Comparing Topgun, what it was in the beginning, what it was when I was a student and then an instructor, and to what it is now, in some ways nothing has changed at Topgun, and in some ways everything has changed at Topgun. What hasn't changed is the responsibility of delivering the most effective briefing and debriefing techniques that aviation has.
>
> Topgun's responsibility is to create teachers and flight leaders to train pilots to go to war. But, if you think about it, the environment has changed so much since 1969. The aircraft are different, world situation is different, the missions, weapon systems, there have been massive advances in how aircraft operate, and of expectations of what aircraft can contribute to the battlefield.

AICs receive graduate-level specialty training that they are then expected to pass on to their teammates.

Another noteworthy change in the Topgun program is the fact that it doesn't stop once a student "graduates." Once a year, usually in the fall, Topgun hosts a "postgraduate" program. It's known as strike fighter tactics refresher course (or "Re-Blue," referring to the "Blue Team," a designation students get upon first entering Topgun). Here, active-duty SFTIs return to Fallon for a two-day refresher, where they receive the latest updates and use them in sorties.

Topgun also conducts an adversary training course, where select pilots from the Navy and Marine Corps adversary squadrons receive individual instruction in all aspects of adversary tactics.

In addition, Topgun features large-scale exercises, known as Integrated and Advanced Training Phases, that can involve as many as fifty aircraft, including carrier wings whose crews receive academic and flight training.

Lieutenant Colonel
Dave Berke, USMC (Ret.),

Former Topgun Pilot and Instructor

Lieutenant Colonel Dave Berke has had an extraordinary military career. A decorated Marine Corps officer, his distinguished career includes that of fighter pilot, Forward Air Controller, and Topgun instructor, among other achievements. He served two tours of duty as an F/A-18 pilot stationed on the carrier USS *John C. Stennis* in support of combat operations in Afghanistan and Iraq. He was assigned as a FAC with the US Army's 1st Armored Division, working alongside SEAL Team Three's Task Unit Bruiser unit, and other units during the harrowing Battle of Ramadi in 2006. He was the only Marine to be selected to fly the F-22 Raptor, and he was the first operational pilot

Lieutenant Colonel Dave Berke (Ret.).

to be qualified to fly the F-35B Lightning II. He earned his master's degree in international public policy from the Johns Hopkins School of Advanced International Studies with a concentration in strategic studies. Upon his retirement from the Marine Corps, he joined a high-performance leadership consultancy, where he is a leadership instructor, speaker, and strategic advisor. What follows is an interview focusing on his Topgun experiences.

When were you commissioned?
I was commissioned in the summer of 1994 and in the summer of 1997, I got my wings. By the fall of 1998, I checked in with my first squadron, and two years after that I got the notification to go to Topgun.

What did you know of Topgun?
Obviously, everybody in the Marine Corps and Naval Aviation knew about Topgun long before ever flying fighters and all of us had seen the movie. All the Navy and Marine Corps pilots go to the same Navy Flight Training Center in Pensacola. Once you get there, the reality of what it takes to be a pilot, as opposed to what was presented in the Tom Cruise movie, really hits you.

Describe what happened when you were told you had been selected to attend Topgun.
In 2000, I was stationed at Miramar flying F-18 Hornets (a single-seater) and had just completed my certification to be an Air Combat Tactics Instructor when another pilot and I were brought in to our commanding officer's office and told we were going to Topgun.

Insofar as reactions go, you don't want to do a big celebration, but, obviously, it felt good—for me it validated and fulfilled a life's dream to know I was going to Fallon.

What feelings did you have going to Fallon?
I flew my jet from Miramar to Fallon. During that flight I experienced a gamut of emotions—excited, nervous, anxious—but probably the biggest one is the feeling of pressure to perform well and that you know a big responsibility is on your shoulders. You're not just a student. My commander said, "Go to Topgun, learn as much as you can, come back, and train the squadron and be a leader in the squadron."

What was your class like?
I arrived at Topgun in May 2001. As it turned out, it was the last class to graduate Topgun before the terrorist attack on 9/11. At the time, classes lasted six weeks. There were six of us and we all knew each other, some better than most. We didn't have any women members. That came later when I was an instructor, where one of my classes was the first to include women pilots in the program.

Describe the structure of the program you went through.
The structure of the program basically was a week of academics and ground school followed by a week of the 1v1 (one-on-one) dogfight flying phase. This is followed by a week and a half of the section (two plane) phase, then about a week and a half of the four-plane phase, called the division phase. Finally, we had some large force exercises, air-to-ground with some escort fighter strikes where you go in and drop your ordnance and fight your way out, that kind of thing. All told it worked out to be six weeks.

What was that first full day like?
I remember that first day, getting that big stack of books—while no one thing stood out, what hit me was that there was a lot to do in a short time. What I remember that did stand out was the high level of professionalism at every level from the most junior to the commanding officer. It was something very palpable the moment you arrived at Topgun. Obviously, with everyone there having a Type A personality, we pushed each other hard, but we did it in order to do our best. There were times you were on your own, doing your own things. Then there were times you were doing things collectively. Sometimes you're struggling, and you need help; other times you're the one giving help. Anytime I asked for help, or anytime anyone else asked for help, the response was always, "Yes."

Lieutenant Colonel Dave Berke flying in formation somewhere in the airspace over NAS Fallon.

DAVE BERKE, USMC (RET.)

What was your first flight like?

The very first flight you make at Topgun is a familiarization flight where you fly over the area and get familiar with landmarks and other topographical features where you'll be training. It's called a 1v0. I remember my first 1v0 flight well, it was an instructional flight called the Offensive BFM (Basic Fighter Maneuvers) ride. You're set up in an offensive position, which means you're flying behind the instructor ready to attack and are about to run through various dogfighting scenarios that you've studied and were in your flight briefing earlier that day. It was just appalling, by far the worst flight I had ever had as a pilot.

We'd get into position and wait for the "fights on" signal from the instructor. When we got it, the next thing I knew, the instructor had reversed course on me, got at my six, and shot me. He did this on numerous occasions. When the mission concluded, we flew back to base. As our planes were re-fueling the instructor told me not to get out of my flight gear. We were going right back up because it had been so bad. This was called an "Immediate Re-Fly" and it was definitely a humbling, eye-opening experience. Such situations are not uncommon. What it pointed out to me was that I was *waaay* behind where I needed to be as a pilot.

I never had to do another Re-Fly after that, which was great. Some guys do, some guys don't. On the second flight, I felt much more comfortable and was able to manage the exercises more effectively, enough so that I was able to identify my mistakes and complete every flight after that.

What were your instructors like?

The Topgun instructors, the way they briefed, the way they flew, they revealed to me that I wasn't anywhere near as good as I needed to be, and not anywhere near as good as them. I never got past that feeling during the entire time I was a student. The most impressive of my instructors was Major David "Crusoe" Robinson, or "Cru." He was a Marine instructor and one of the two senior instructors there. Cru was the most accomplished, most professional, most capable officer I had ever seen in my career. I got to do a number of flights with him at Topgun, and while all the instructors were impressive, he stood out above and beyond the others.

What happened after you returned to your squadron?

I returned to my squadron, VMFA-314, the "Black Knights," in July 2001. That's when the huge responsibility of being a Topgun trained pilot really hit. My commander tasked me with training all the things I had learned and would have an impact on the squadron. Then, a little over two months later, 9/11 happened and the squadron was sent off to war. Now, lessons that had been theoretical, were tangible.

What sort of missions did you perform in the Global War on Terror aftermath of 9/11?

We were based on the carrier USS *John C. Stennis* (CVN 74). The majority of our missions were interdiction missions, a lot of air-to-ground, working with Forward Air Controllers (FACs). I dropped some bombs, got shot at. It was during this deployment to Afghanistan when I got word that I was going to be a Topgun instructor.

Did you have an idea you might be asked to be an instructor?

The day before I left Topgun as a student, Crusoe pulled me aside and asked me if I was interested in being a Topgun instructor. There was much more to the selection process for Topgun instructors, of course, but he wanted to know from me my interest in coming back. At the time I took it as a compliment, told him so, but since he didn't make any commitment, I left it at that.

Then, when I was on the carrier, I got an email from him inviting me to be an instructor. My answer was, "Of course." I still had to finish my deployment flying missions to Afghanistan, but now I knew that my next duty assignment would take me to Fallon where I would apply lessons learned in actual combat to courses at Fallon. And, training when I became an instructor reflected those recent experiences in combat.

What do you consider are the high points of your military career?

I was pretty lucky. As a Topgun instructor, I was responsible for developing counter-tactics against missile attack. I was part of the group that developed the Navy and Marine Corps defense against Iraqi SAM threats during Operation Iraqi Freedom, which was a really cool experience. In 2002, I got qualified to fly the F-16 Fighting Falcon. Thanks to Topgun I got to fly the F-22 Raptor through an exchange program with the Air Force. At the time the requirement was that only people who had been Topgun instructors were allowed to fly it. And, later I got to fly the F-35 Lightning II. Thanks to Topgun I got to do a whole bunch of things that nobody else got to do, and make a real impact to Naval Aviation.

Lieutenant Colonel Dave Berke conducting maneuvers somewhere in the airspace over NAS Fallon.

16 // TOP GUN 2: MAVERICK

Though rumors of a *Top Gun* sequel percolated for years following the movie's successful run, such talk was more tease than truth—until 2010, when Paramount Pictures got the original movie's producer, Jerry Bruckheimer, and director, Tony Scott, on board. Tom Cruise was soon brought in as well; as originally conceived in the first draft of the screenplay, however, his Maverick role would be minor. The story would emphasize a dynamic that was different from the original's "go-it-alone" pilot clashing with squadron mates and authority. An important part of that rationale came from director Scott himself, who stated that he did not want to do a straight remake.

Also, today's military environment is vastly different from that of 1986. For one, we noted in the opening chapter that the F-14 Tomcat was arguably as much a star in the original movie as Tom Cruise. The Tomcat was retired by the Navy in 2006 after thirty-two years of service; it was replaced by the F/A-18 Hornet and Super Hornet and the stealthy F-35 Lightning II Joint Strike Fighter—and, even more recently, by drones.

Additionally, the threat has significantly changed. Consigned to the dustbin of history is the Soviet Union, the primary (if unstated) villain in the original. The background conflict for *Top Gun 2: Maverick* is described as a mix of fifth-generation fighters and drone technology. If that's the case, it certainly provides a role for the Navy's F-32 squaring off against Russia with its Sukhoi Su-57 stealth air superiority fighter; or China with its Shenyang J-31

Navy fighter pilots. He added, "There is an amazing role for Maverick in the movie and there is no *Top Gun* without Maverick, and it is going to be Maverick playing Maverick."

The story will reflect the fact that thirty years have passed. Publicity photos revealed that Maverick is now a captain—a fact that those who served in the Navy have pointed out must be inaccurate. Technically, a naval officer with thirty-plus years of service should have an admiral's rank; a captain would have been forced to retire much earlier. But, as Scott himself famously said of complaints of military inaccuracy in *Top Gun*, "We're not making this movie for fighter pilots, we're making it for Kansas wheat farmers who don't know the difference."

One part of the story will reflect the state of today's Navy accurately: the rise of drone use in warfare and the decline of human fighter pilots, which of course changes the nature of aerial combat. Ellison observed, "When you look at the world of dogfighting, what's interesting about it is that it's not a world that exists to the same degree when the original movie came out." He added, it's a world "where it's drone technology and fifth-generation fighters," and the sequel will be "exploring the end of an era of dogfighting and pilots and what the culture is today."

One thing that's for sure, as people who've seen the movie know: Maverick's backseater, Goose, can't return (rumors of the "ghost of Goose" making an appearance notwithstanding). But, his son, who appeared sitting on the piano in the original, can—and does. *Only the Brave* star Miles Teller has been tapped for the role; according to reports, his character carries a chip on his shoulder, blaming Maverick for his father's death.

Jennifer Connelly is slated to be the new leading lady in the movie, rumored to be playing "Penny Benjamin," the admiral's daughter Maverick chased in the original movie.

News of cast additions in August 2018, most notably those of Ed Harris and John Hamm, was overshadowed by Paramount's announcement that it had pushed back the release date of *Top Gun 2: Maverick* to late June 2020. The news was met with shock and disappointment by fans eager to see the film. According to the studio, their reasoning was

LEFT: Jerry Bruckheimer.

BELOW: Miles Teller.

multirole, twin-engine stealth fighter; or various drones from both countries. And, since this is Hollywood, they can make any type of drone they want. Against such a rich threatboard scenario, the sky's the limit when it comes to potential adversaries in *Top Gun 2: Maverick*.

That sky all but came crashing down in 2012 with Tony Scott's suicide. Production remained in doubt in the immediate wake of the director's death. But with Bruckheimer still on board, and with successive drafts of the script that pushed Cruise forward into a starring role, the sequel was only delayed, not dropped.

Reflecting the evolution of the script, four writers have been involved with its development: Peter Craig, Justin Marks, Ashley Edward Miller, and Zack Stentz. Skydance Media, together with Bruckheimer, is producing *Top Gun 2: Maverick* for Paramount. In a 2015 interview, David Ellison, Skydance's CEO, observed that Justin Marks "has a phenomenal take to really update" the world of today's

ABOVE: Jennifer Connelly.

RIGHT: The underside of an F/A-18 Super Hornet showing its weapons load. In *Top Gun 2: Maverick*, it, the F-35 Lightning II, and drones have replaced the iconic F-14 Tomcat of *Top Gun* fame, having been retired from service in 2006.

to give filmmakers extra time to work out the logistics of presenting flight sequences with new technology, fighters, and drones. It's an expensive decision, but one that stands to reason given how important the flying sequences were in the original.

And, as in the first *Top Gun* movie, US Navy participation includes use of one of its aircraft carriers, in this case the nuclear-powered supercarrier USS *Abraham Lincoln*. In the summer of 2018, a fifteen-person crew from Paramount Pictures and Bruckheimer Films spent a week aboard the Norfolk-based carrier to shoot footage of flight deck air operations, and take-offs and landings of F/A-18 Super Hornets from Carrier Air Wing Seven the "Freedom Fighters" as part of their carrier qualifications. Paramount stated it "will reimburse the Navy for any costs incurred for flying sequences which do not meet training objectives."

Though the studio remained mum on the subject, the "other" flying sequences likely were revealed on the official Facebook page of VFA-125, the "Rough Raiders." Carrier crewmembers posted videos of flights of F-35 Lightning II stealth multirole fighters flying in formation over the carrier. And, in flights reminiscent of the famous "buzzing the tower" sequence in the original, video showed two F-35s making similar runs forming vapor cones and high-speed passes on afterburner as they flew past the carrier's island.

Of the Navy's participation, Commander Dave Hecht, public affairs officer with Naval Air Force Atlantic, said in a statement, "*Top Gun* inspired countless men and women to volunteer to protect and defend our country as naval aviators, and the crew of USS *Abraham Lincoln* are excited to play a small role in bringing this story back to the silver screen and inspiring another generation to serve in the world's finest Navy."

Another leak was a tantalizing photo that surfaced on the fan sites www.RevengeOfTheFans.com and www.WeGotThisCovered.com that showed a Navy F/A-18 Super Hornet with special paint and markings that included the name Capt. Pete Mitchell "Maverick." The silhouettes of three aircraft were stenciled on the right cockpit rail, along with the Topgun seal on its tail, further adding credence to the rumors that Cruise's character is an instructor at Naval Air Warfighting Development Center at NAS Fallon.

Thanks to social media, such nuggets will continue to surface, adding interest and excitement for *Top Gun 2: Maverick*. Such clips of flight operations will also reinforce something Dave Baranek noted that added important verisimilitude to the original. Baranek was a Navy lieutenant and Topgun instructor who participated in the production of *Top Gun*. When asked about the movie, he said in an interview, "I'm glad they showed the hard parts. The movie doesn't glamorize the training. And the students are tense. It's a highly competitive situation."

"Maverick is not just a maverick. He does things differently, that's all. The conflict in the movie and his behavior show that he's good," he said. "The Topgun instructors' job is to develop, to take off the rough edges."

In *Top Gun 2: Maverick*, Tom Cruise does exactly that. Differently.

INDEX

IMAGE CREDITS

Alamy Stock Photos: 8 (Ronald Grant Archive), 10 (Collection Christophel), 11 (Moviestore Collection Ltd), 13 (Entertainment Pictures), 14 (Ronald Grant Archive), 15 (Moviestore Collection Ltd), 16 (Paramount Pictures/Ronald Grant Archive/Mary Evans), 19 (United Archives GmbH), 36 (Moviestore Collection Ltd), 44 (The Advertising Archives), 45 (Keystone Pictures USA), 50 (History and Art Collection), 73 right (Chronicle), 81 (PF-(sdasm3)), 87 top (Richard P Long), 87 bottom (Malcolm Haines), 96 (SPUTNIK), 99 bottom (Radu Nedici), 104 (Chronicle), 105 (Sueddeutsche Zeitung Photo), 107 bottom (Alto Vintage Images), 108 left (Aviation History Collection), 108 middle (Mim Friday), 108 right (Sueddeutsche Zeitung Photo), 110 (Peter Lane), 111 top left (Aviation History Collection), 116 (Everett Collection Inc), 117 top left (Pictorial Press Ltd), 129 (Kevin Griffin), 131 (PF-(aircraft)), 137 top (PJF Military Collection), 156 left (MediaPunch Inc), 156 right (Tsuni / USA), 157 right (Image Press Agency). **Lt. Col. Dave Berke:** 150–151, 153. **Creative Commons:** 72 (Noop1958, CCA 3.0), 124 (Marc Grossman, CCA 3.0), 126 (Casey17, CCA 3.0). **Getty Images:** 62 (Hulton Archive), 68 top (Bettmann), 133 (John B. Carnett), 155 (Jamie McCarthy). **Library of Congress:** 39 right, 41 left, 42 right, 43 left, 46, 63, 64 right, 65 both, 66–67, 70 both, 71 left, 73 left, 107 top. **Motorbooks Archive:** 17, 39 left and middle, 40 bottom left (both), 41 center (both) and right, 42 left (all), 48–50, 71 right. **NASA:** 59, 132. **US Air Force:** 34, 40 top, 43 right, 55 left, 56–58, 60–61, 64 left, 68 bottom, 69, 77–79, 80 right, 82, 84 left, 86, 89–91, 103, 106 both, 109, 111 bottom, 113, 128, 130, 134, 135 (Staff Sgt. Aaron Allmon II), 136, 137 bottom, 140 right, 141–142. **US Navy:** 5 (Photographer's Mate 2nd Class Jayme Pastoric), 7 (Photographer's Mate 2nd Class Daniel J. McLain), 20, 29–33, 38, 47, 52, 54, 55 right, 74, 76, 80 left, 85, 92–95, 97, 98 both, 99 top, 100–102, 112, 114–115, 117 top right and bottom, 118–123, 125, 127, 139, 140 left, 143–149, 154, 157 bottom.